BASHŌ'S NARROW ROAD

THE ROCK SPRING COLLECTION OF JAPANESE LITERATURE

Bashō's Narrow Road

SPRING & AUTUMN PASSAGES

Narrow Road to the Interior
AND THE RENGA SEQUENCE
A Farewell Gift to Sora

TWO WORKS BY MATSUO BASHŌ

TRANSLATED FROM THE JAPANESE,
WITH ANNOTATIONS, BY

Hiroaki Sato

FOREWORD BY

Cor van den Heuvel

STONE BRIDGE PRESS • *Berkeley, California*

Published by

Stone Bridge Press, P.O, Box 8208, Berkeley, CA 94707

510-524-8732 • sbp@netcom.com • www.stonebridge.com

Cover design by Linda Thurston.

Text design by Peter Goodman.

Text copyright © 1996 by Hiroaki Sato.

Signature of the author on front part-title page: "Bashō."

Illustrations by Yosa Buson reproduced by permission of Itsuō Museum.

LIBRARY OF CONGRESS CATALOGING-IN-PUBLICATION DATA

Matsuo, Bashō, 1644–1694.
    [Oku no hosomichi. English]
    Bashō's Narrow road: spring and autumn passages: two works / by
Matsuo Bashō: translated from the Japanese, with annotations by
Hiroaki Sato.
        p.   cm.
    Includes bibliographical references and index.
    Contents: Narrow road to the interior and the renga sequence—A
farewell gift to Sora.
    ISBN 1-880656-20-5 (pbk.)
    1. Matsuo, Bashō, 1644–1694—Journeys—Japan. 2. Japan—
Description and travel—Early works to 1800. 3. Authors, Japanese—
Edo period, 1600–1868—Journeys—Japan. I. Satō, Hiroaki, 1942–.
II. Matsuo, Bashō, 1644–1694. Sora sen. English. III. Title.
PL794.4.Z5A3613   1996
895.6'132–dc20   96-4392
                                                        CIP

THIS BOOK IS DEDICATED TO

Miss Eleanor Wolff
(September 23, 1907–October 26, 1995)

Doris Bargen

CONTENTS

Foreword   9

Preface   13

Introduction   17

NARROW ROAD TO THE INTERIOR

Bashō's Route, with Major
Stopping Places   38

Narrow Road to the Interior   41

Endnotes   134

A FAREWELL GIFT TO SORA

Prefatory Note   158

A Farewell Gift to Sora   160

Commentary   166

Index of Poets   185

FOREWORD

CARRYING A PACK WITH HIS WRITING MATERIALS, A FEW pieces of clothing, and several gifts from friends who saw him off, the poet Bashō set out on a hike to the wilds of northern Honshū in the spring of 1689. With his close disciple Sora, he planned to visit places famous as wonders of nature or significant in literary, religious, or military history—and he wanted to spread to the poetry lovers he would meet in the towns and villages along the way his methods of writing renga, the communal linked verse that was his passion and greatest concern in life.

The account he wrote of that trip, and which he revised and polished for four years, is one of the masterpieces of Japanese literature. Called *Oku no Hosomichi*, this travel diary is in a genre called *haibun*—a mixture of haiku-like prose and haiku. Though he had done a number of shorter works in this genre—about other travels, places he had lived, and people he had known—this was his longest and best. He died not long after he finished it, while on still another journey.

The work is shorter than many Western novellas: a small pond compared with the vast ocean of Lady Murasaki's eleventh-century novel *Genji Monogatari* (The Tale of Genji), another major constellation in Japan's literary firmament. But it is smaller only in size. In fact, part of its greatness lies in its doing so much with so little. Like a haiku it gets its vivid immediacy and sensory power from the suggestiveness created by its terse, laconic style. It is all at once a travel journal *(kikōbun)*, a haibun, a renga, and a haiku anthology. Bashō deliberately shaped it this way—changing the order of some of the events and even inventing some—to make it a work of art.

It follows the general form of Bashō's style of renga (known as *haikai no renga*): from the slow, low-key introduction to the varied development of the middle part to the fast close of the finale. Though it is more unified and thematic than renga, it still has many surprising renga-like juxtapositions provided by places and events—not only those he experienced or invented, but also many he evokes from allusions to or quotations from historical, literary, and mythical sources. These elements move in and out of the prose and haiku.

One could even describe this haibun as a series of about fifty short haibun which work with each other much like the links in a renga. The haiku themselves present a varied array that also moves from subject to subject in the disjunctive manner of renga: from the hidden blossoms of a chestnut growing close to the eaves, to the ghostly dreams of dead warriors in the summer grass, to the poet trying to sleep while lying next to a pissing horse, to the rain-flooded Mogami River, a faint moon over Mount Haguro, the Milky Way over a rough ocean, and the cry of a cricket coming from under an ancient helmet in a provincial shrine.

Haiku, then known as *hokku*, were just beginning to be treated as separate poems around Bashō's time. Before that they were each simply the beginning link of a renga. Paradoxically, since they could now exist as poems separate from the renga, they could also now be combined with prose to create haibun. There was a centuries-old precedent for this. The tanka—a poem almost twice as long as a haiku, thirty-one syllables versus seventeen—had long been combined with prose in various kinds of literary works. *Genji*, which mixes eight hundred tanka with its prose, is only one of countless examples of stories, tales, and travel diaries that combined poetry with prose before Bashō. Haibun can refer to the haiku-style prose by itself, and haiku poets sometimes write haibun without any haiku.

Bashō had been developing his haiku and his travel-journal haibun for a number of years. His earlier haibun, such as *Nozarashi Kikō,* tend to have the haiku just tacked on to the prose; the two are not integrated and working together. Nor is the prose as developed into a haiku style as in his later works. The combining of haiku and prose into a totally unified work of art found its culmination in the *Oku*.

In this remarkable translation by Hiroaki Sato, we find the elliptical, allusive, suggestive richness of the original brought over into English. The idiosyncratic lightness of style combined with the passionate intensity of love evinced by Bashō for past poets and their poetry, the exploits of legendary gods, goddesses, heroes and heroines and the places hallowed by their deeds or presence, and the natural wonders of the land all come alive in this new translation. Without Bashō's knowledge of the literary, legendary, and real history of Japan, we may not recognize what, for us, is locked up in the *Oku*. This is where Mr. Sato's annotations step in and unlock and shed light on many of the innumerable references Bashō has packed into his work. They work together with the translation to make this the most accessible version in English.

The annotations not only reveal the many allusions to earlier works but present us with the works themselves, for Mr. Sato has added them, or excerpts, to many of these notes in both Japanese transliteration and in English translation. He also gives us the continuations of a number of the renga Bashō participated in on this journey, where in the haibun itself the poet has given us only the opening hokku. These added links elucidate Bashō's linking techniques and give us a sense of the renga parties he took part in by indicating the interplay between the poets. All of these notes (footnotes and endnotes) open up the whole work like a program in a computer opens windows in one part of a file into other related files, and from those into still others. We can follow many of the threads Bashō used in his work back to their original sources and then back again to see how he wove them into his own unique creation.

One of the most rewarding of these avenues, threads, or files, that stream from and into the original *Oku no Hosomichi* is Mr. Sato's complete translation, with commentary, of *A Farewell Gift to Sora*, a renga written toward the end of the journey by Bashō, Sora, and Hokushi. It retains various links they considered, discussed, and rejected, along with many of Bashō's comments on these and on the accepted links, and on writing renga in general. So we have the *Oku* branching out to the *Gift* branching out to the picture we get of the poets sitting together writing the renga.

And the renga itself is a marvelous progression of interrelated images that leap from one setting to another in the sharply disjunctive mode typical of the best linked verse. From swallows flying south, to a traveler riding a horse through a distant field of flowers, to an argument at a wrestling match, to otters jumping into a river, and on and on to the wild and crazy poet at the end ringing a temple bell at dusk with flowers falling all around him. Our minds go surfing from the rich panorama of the haibun itself out through this dazzling renga for an exhilarating ride unmatched by anything to be found on the Internet.

COR VAN DEN HEUVEL
Editor, *The Haiku Anthology*

PREFACE

THIS TRANSLATION WAS PROMPTED BY "WHERE HAIKU AND Music Meet," a series of three concerts of the piano music that Kashiwagi Toshio composed for seventeen haiku (hokku) from *Oku no Hosomichi*. The concerts were held in May 1994 in New York to mark the three hundredth anniversary of Bashō's death—at the Bruno Walter Auditorium of the New York Public Library, the Japan Society, and the Nippon Club—with Mr. Kashiwagi attending each session and Clara Chieko Inaba playing the piano. Excerpts from the travel account in my translation were made part of the program notes. Later in the same year Mr. Kashiwagi, who studied with Klaus Pringsheim before the war, died, at age eighty-two.

A Farewell Gift to Sora was originally published in *One Hundred Frogs: From Renga to Haiku to English* (Weatherhill, 1983). I have revised it for inclusion here.

Yosa Buson (1716–83), a poet and painter who admired Bashō, is believed to have copied and illustrated *Oku no Hosomichi* at least ten times. The illustrations here are taken from the ones he did toward the end of 1779.

In this book all Japanese names are given the Japanese way, family name first, with the exceptions of Nobuyuki Yuasa and me. By custom Japanese poets and artists from certain periods are better known by their personal names, which are more often noms de plume than not. For example, the real, full name of the person we normally identify as Bashō is Matsuo Munefusa—Munefusa being one of his personal adult names. Bashō, "plantain," is the pen name this poet adopted in 1682, when he was thirty-eight years old. He had at least fifteen other pen names, the best-known of which is Tōsei, "peach-blue/green," which he adopted in 1675, when he was thirty-one. Though he started publishing hokku under the name of Munefusa, only scholars will recognize it as Bashō's real name.

The calendar used is lunar, not solar.

I have translated place names where their surface meanings have direct associations or are punned upon. In each such case, I have given the original, Japanese name in the note.

Unless otherwise noted, all translations quoted are mine.

Oku no Hosomichi is included in countless texts, many of them closely annotated. Annotations such as those given to classics like this travel account are based on knowledge accumulated through generations of scholarly investigation, and the notes given to the three texts I have consulted for this translation, listed immediately below, differ from one another mainly in emphasis, except where new material or speculation has turned up. Most of the information I give in my notes derives from these annotators.

Also, a number of Bashō's hokku come with variants, including orthographic variants. This is because he wrote hokku during renga sessions, in letters, on *shikishi* ("poem cards"), and on paintings, sometimes writing the same hokku on several occasions. In addition, he revised a number of hokku. Bashō scholars normally list all such variants, dating them where possible.

On account of this, as well as the ready availability of various texts, I do not cite specific sources in my notes.

Ebara Taizō and Ogata Tsutomu. *Oku no Hosomichi.* Kadokawa Shoten, 1967. With detailed commentary on each hokku; includes a translation into modern Japanese and excerpts from Sora's diary.

Sakamoto Gen and Shiraishi Teizō. *Oku no Hosomichi.* Kōdansha, 1975. Includes a translation into modern Japanese and an anthology of modern writings inspired by some of the places Bashō and Sora visited.

Sugiura Shōichirō *et al. Bashō Bunshū.* Iwanami Shoten, 1959. Includes Bashō's other travel diaries, haibun, and letters.

In my notes, I cite poems from some of the "twenty-one imperial anthologies of Japanese poems," compiled from the early tenth to the mid-fifteenth century. Any title that ends with *shū,* "collection," and comes with no explanation refers to one of them, though this excludes *Man'yō Shū,* the oldest extant anthology of Japanese poems, which is believed to have taken its present form in the early ninth century. A full listing of the twenty-one anthologies is found in my translation, *String of Beads: Complete Poems of Princess Shikishi* (University of Hawaii Press, 1993), pp. 163–65.

In preparing this annotated translation, I have also consulted the following texts:

Imoto Nōichi and Hori Nobuo. *Bashō Shū: Zen.* Shūei Sha, 1970. Complete writings by Bashō, with minimum annotations.

Muramatsu Tomotsugu. *Bashō no Sakuhin to Denki no Kenkyū.* Kasama Shoin, 1977. Contains three *dempon,* "transmitted texts," compared line by line.

Nose Tomoji. *Renga Geijutsu no Seikaku.* Kadokawa Shoten, 1970. Contains a detailed commentary on *Sora Sen* (A Farewell Gift to Sora).

Ogiwara Yasuo. *Bashō Shokan Shū.* Iwanami Shoten, 1976. A collection of letters, annotated.

Okada Rihei. *Oku no Hosomichi: Gakan.* Kyoto: Yutaka Shobō, 1973. With a reproduction of a text copied and illustrated by Buson.

Ōtani Tokuzō and Nakamura Shujō. *Bashō Kushū.* Iwanami Shoten, 1962. Annotates about 85 percent of all the hokku attributed to Bashō and some of the renga in which he took part.

Shimasue Kiyoshi. *Bashō Renku Zen-chūkai,* V and VI. Shō'ō Sha, 1981. Contains renga composed during the journey, with comments.

Yamamoto Satoshi. *Bashō: Oku no Hosomichi Jiten*. Kōdansha, 1994. A report by a modern traveler who retraced the paths that Bashō and Sora took step by step.

Nancy Rossiter and Robert Fagan helped revise the translations and commentary at the draft stage. Doris Bargen, who suggested translating the whole of *Oku no Hosomichi*, and Cor van den Heuvel read the initial version, with Haiku Master Cor also writing the Foreword.

Finally, Kyoko I. Selden read the version revised by them and pointed out a large number of interpretative errors and inconsistencies. My indebtedness to her is unfathomable.

INTRODUCTION

IN 1689 MATSUO BASHŌ (1644–94), ACCOMPANIED BY HIS friend Kawai Sora (1649–1710), made a five-month-long journey. Starting out from Edo (today's Tokyo) at the end of the third month, he went north as far as Hiraizumi, in Rikuzen (Iwate), then moved to the Japan Sea and traveled southwest along the coast. When he reached Tsuruga Port, north of Kyoto, he turned southeast. His trip ended in Ōgaki, in Mino (Gifu), where he arrived on the twenty-first or the twenty-third of the eighth month.

The trek covered 1,985 kilometers or 1,233 miles—roughly the distance from the southern tip of Florida to Connecticut as the crow flies. The account known as *Oku no Hosomichi*, here translated as "Narrow Road to the Interior," is Bashō's description of the journey. Though brief, it is among the most celebrated works of Japanese literature.

Life with No Fixed Abode

Bashō was on the road for much of his last ten years, making similar journeys to various places. The one to the north was the most arduous and, because of the masterful account he left of it, the most famous. Why did he decide to devote himself to such travels?

The immediate impetus was apparently the great fire that struck Edo toward the end of 1682. It engulfed Bashō's house, forcing him to "submerge himself in the tide [of the Sumida River] and cover himself with a sedge mat [to fend off the heat] in order to survive in the smoke," as Takarai Kikaku (1661–1707) put it in his tribute to his deceased master. The disaster literally made him realize the truth of the Buddhist assertion that life is like "a house on fire," that there really is "no fixed abode" in this world, Kikaku said. Certainly, Bashō's restless wanderings began early in the following year.

Uta-Makura and "Poetic Truth"

But such a philosophical conclusion about life does not adequately explain Bashō's dogged visits to various places that followed. Judging from the places he selected and what he did during his travels, Bashō aimed to achieve two goals, one spiritual, the other practical. The spiritual goal has to do with "poetic truth." He expressed it in *Oi no Kobumi* (Brief Epistle on the Travel Casket), an account of his six-month wandering from 1687 to 1688:

> Heels torn, I am the same as Saigyō, and I think of him at the Tenryū ferry. Renting a horse, I conjure up in my mind the sage who became furious. In the beautiful spectacles of the mountain, field, ocean, and coast, I see the achievements of the Creation. Or I follow the trails left by those who, completely unattached, pursued the Way, or I try to fathom the truth expressed by those with poetic sensibility.

Saigyō (1118–89) was a traveling poet-priest whom Bashō greatly admired, and the story he was recalling has to do with the priest being insulted and whipped by insolent samurai on an over-crowded ferryboat but accepting it as part of his Buddhist training. "The sage" refers to Shōkū, who legend says lost his temper in an accident involving a groom and, terribly embarrassed by his own unsaintly vituperation, fled the scene. For our purpose, in any case, the most important part of the paragraph is the last phrase: *fuzei no hito no makoto o ukagau,* "fathom the truth expressed by those with poetic sensibility."

In Japan, where the first large-scale collection of verse dates from the eighth century, a great many places were routinely described or mentioned in poetry from the outset, and many of these came to be known as *uta-makura,* "poetic pillows." Uta-makura then acquired the same significance as *kidai* or *kigo*, "seasonal subjects" or "topics," each representing a certain idea or sentiment or a trigger thereof. For Bashō the purpose of visiting such places was, as he said to Kikaku in a letter, *furuki uta-domo no makoto o kan(zu)*—to "feel the truth of old poems." His passion in this regard was intense. Once, in 1688, he walked 160 mountainous miles in five days so that he might see the full moon at one particular "poetic pillow"—in this instance Mount Obasute, where in the legendary past old women are said to have been abandoned to save food.

As he learned during his travels to the north, many uta-makura existed in name only, and barely that. Shirakawa Barrier, mentioned at the start of his account, is a case in point. Built in the province of Iwashiro (today's Fukushima), it was originally a fort or stockade against *Emishi*, the northern "barbarians" to those inhabiting the southern part of the land. A few centuries later it apparently fell into disuse. By the eleventh century it had become an uta-makura that was supposed to evoke the sense that it was where civilization and culture ended and what Joseph Conrad might have called "the heart of darkness" began. Priest Nōin (b. 988) wrote a poem:

> When I went down to Michinokuni, I made this
> poem at Shirakawa Barrier:
>
> *Miyako o ba kasumi to tomo ni tachishikado akikaze zo fuku*
> *Shirakawa no Seki*
> Though I left the City with haze rising, autumn wind
> blows at Shirakawa Barrier

Selected for the travel section of the fourth imperial anthology *Go-Shūi Shū*, compiled in 1086, this tanka, or thirty-one-syllable verse, would become the most famous poem describing this uta-makura, requiring later poets to recall it when they made their own on the subject. For example, *Azuma Kagami* (History of the East), put together toward the end of the thirteenth century, cites a poem that the warrior-poet Kajiwara Kagesue (1162–1200) made in

1189 when Minamoto no Yoritomo (1147–99)[1] led an army to vanquish Fujiwara no Yasuhira (d. 1189) who had, at Yoritomo's own instigation, killed Yoritomo's brother Yoshitsune (1159–89).[2] On the twenty-ninth of the seventh month of that year:

> [Yoritomo] crossed Shirakawa Barrier. He dedicated white silk cloth to the barrier deity. While doing this, he summoned Kagesue and said, "This is early autumn. Don't you recall Priest Nōin's old poem?" Kagesue reined in his horse and recited a poem:
>
> *Akikaze ni kusaki no tsuyu o harawasete kimi ga koyureba sekimori mo nashi*
>
> Making the autumn wind sweep dew from grass and trees, you, milord, cross, with no barrier guards

When Bashō visited the site of Shirakawa Barrier in 1689, it is doubtful that even a trace of its ruins remained. All that he and his companion Sora were able to do, it appears, was to pay their respects to a shrine that a local inn proprietor said housed the barrier deity. Whether it was the same shrine that *Azuma Kagami* mentions is not certain, either. This may explain why in crossing the place Bashō readily remembered some of the more famous poems incorporating the poetic place name but could not describe anything like a barrier or a fort.

The Sequential Poetic Form: Renga or Linked Verse

The other, and more practical, goal of Bashō's journeys was to solidify and spread his influence as a poet. Today the notion of a poet traveling to establish his influence may appear somewhat strange. In Bashō's day, when a poet could make a living as a paid teacher, doing so was accepted, at times even essential. This was particularly true in

---

1   The founder of the first warrior government, Kamakura Bakufu.

2   One of Japan's most illustrious military commanders. The English historian James Murdoch once called him "Japan's Napoleon." For an account of his life, see Hiroaki Sato, *Legends of the Samurai* (New York: Overlook Press, 1995), pp. 110–56.

Bashō's case because he worked with the sequential poetic form of *renga*, "linked verse," and its offshoot, the *hokku*, its opening unit.

The renga was born in the thirteenth century from the tendency of the 5–7–5–7–7-syllable tanka to split into two parts, 5–7–5 and 7–7, and from the Japanese poets' propensity to turn poetry composition into a group game. At first the two split parts, 5–7–5 and 7–7 syllables, were composed by two persons. Then they began to be linked together alternately, indefinitely. In the end the standard length of a hundred parts was set, which was most often composed by half a dozen or more people. What we know today as haiku started out as the opening unit or line of this sequential form: hence its original name, the hokku, "the opening phrase."

Renga composition was essentially—and remains—a game with multiple participants. Consequently, rules were made, and these in time grew to be what are probably the most complex rules ever devised for any poetic form. And their complexity, along with the delight the Japanese people took in composing verse in and as a group, led to the arrangement in which a *sōshō*, "master," or *tenja*, "point-giver" (judge), would preside over each session as a guide and teacher. Such a master earned payment for this and also for evaluating submitted renga and hokku. That is how most masters made a living. Indeed, one term for holding a renga session was *kōgyō*, which carries with it a suggestion of a business enterprise.

Bashō, however, began to avoid seeking payments for his pedagogic role in his late thirties, choosing to live on donations from his wealthier friends and students. Pecuniary recompense jarred his search for poetic truth. He made this most clear when he wrote to the samurai poet Suganuma Kyokusui (d. 1717). In his letter dated the eighteenth of the second month, 1692, he divided *haikai*[3] practitioners into three categories:

When it comes to the way of poetry[4] there are generally

---

3   See pp. 24–26 for a definition of haikai.

4   *Fūga no michi.*

three grades of people, as I see it. There are those who run around, trying day and night to make points, vying to win, with no attempt to see the Way. These may be called confused noisemakers in poetry. But because they help fill the stomachs of the wives and children of the judges and replenish the money boxes of their landlords, what they do is better than doing evil things.

Then there are those who, though wealthy, refrain from engaging in ostentatious pleasures. Looking upon haikai writing as better than gossiping about other people, they compose two or three sequences for winning points, day or night, but do not boast when they win, nor become angry even when they lose. Whatever may happen, they at once set out to work out a new sequence and try to come up with clever ideas during the brief space of time that an incense stick five *bu*[5] long takes to burn. When it's finished they delight in the points given instantly, just like boys playing cards. These people nevertheless arrange food and provide adequate wine, thereby helping the poor and fattening judges. In that sense they, too, in some way contribute to the establishment of the Way.

Then there are fellows who work hard for the goal of true poetry and soothe their hearts by doing so. These do not easily take to criticizing others and, with the thought that poetry writing is another vehicle for entering the True Way,[6] explore the spirit of Fujiwara no Teika,[7] trace the intent of Saigyō,[8] examine the heart of Lo-t'ien,[9] and enter the mind of Tu Fu[10]—all of the remote past. There

---

5   One *bu* is equal to 0.119 inch. This competitive composition stressed speed. The practice dates from earlier tanka days. Retired Emperor Gotoba (1180–1239) mentions it in his treatise on poetics, *Go-Kuden*.

6   Buddhism.

7   A tanka poet (1162–1241).

8   A tanka poet (1118–89); see p. 18.

9   A Chinese poet also known as Po Chü-yi (772–846).

10   A Chinese poet (712–70).

are so few of these that, the ones in the capital and the ones in the countryside combined, you can readily count them with your ten fingers. You are to be one of those few. It is understandable that you should take great care and work hard at it.

Little wonder then that his letters in the last ten years of his life are sprinkled with emergency requests to "borrow" this or that.

Was Bashō a Ninja?

When a renga master traveled, it was important to have an array of literary-minded merchants, samurai, or other people of means lined up along the way who were willing to accommodate the visiting poet for the pleasure of taking part in a session or two of composing renga. When such people were not available, as apparently happened during some parts of Bashō's travels to the north, the itinerant poet could be reduced to an itinerant pauper.

Here, because several aspects of this famed journey, such as expenses, remain a mystery, I might as well touch on a speculation which, not altogether implausible, was popular for a while, that Bashō might have served as a ninja during his travels to the north.

Bashō was from a former warrior-class family in Iga, Mino (today's Mie), a famous breeding ground for ninja, who were often employed as spies. Just about the time Bashō set out to the north, there was a quiet dispute between an agent of the Tokugawa shogunate and Date Tsunamura (1659–1719), the lord of the Sendai fiefdom, concerning the renovation of the Nikkō shrine. The Nikkō, which Bashō and Sora were to visit in the early part of their travels, was the mausoleum of the founder of the shogunate, Ieyasu (1542–1616), and the cost of the renovation, as estimated by the Date family who were assigned the work, could be ruinous. However, for a local fiefdom to enter a demurer to any Tokugawa order was tantamount to suicide, and the shogunate might have wanted to dispatch a secret agent to look into the matter. There are, in addition, some circumstances that can't be fully explained. Bashō originally had in mind a different traveling companion but switched to

Sora at the last minute. Also, Sora apparently did not leave Edo at the same time Bashō did.

To our disappointment perhaps, the scholar Muramatsu Tomotsugu, after an exhaustive documentary investigation, had to conclude that Sora, not Bashō, might have been given some duties to carry out by the government, but there probably is nothing more to the story.[11]

The speculation that Bashō may have been a ninja arose partly because of a diary that Sora kept during the journey, which was not published until as late as 1943.[12] Such theorization aside, though, this perfunctory recording of day-to-day occurrences has shed a good deal of light on *Oku no Hosomichi*, indicating that Bashō's composition was not a straight "travel account." Bashō reshuffled dates, concocted some poems for Sora, created impressions contrary to what actually happened, and otherwise fabricated for literary effect.

Haikai no Renga

The type of renga Bashō and poets of like mind wrote was categorized as *haikai*, "humorous," to distinguish it from the orthodox variety that closely adhered to the dictates of court poetics. Initially, the renga so termed were *humorous*. To begin with an anomalous example, during one session Sōchō (1448–1532) came up with an innocuous, completely orthodox 7–7:

fuji wa sagarite yūgure no sora
the wisteria droops in the evening sky

To which Sōgi (1421–1502) quickly responded with a 5–7–5:

---

11   Muramatsu Tomotsugu, *Bashō no Sakuhin to Denki no Kenkyū* (Kasama Shoin, 1977), p. 791.

12   According to *Haikai Dai-jiten* (Meiji Shoin, 1957), it was published in full under the title of *Oku no Hosomichi Zuikō Nikki* by Ogawa Shobō with Yamamoto Yasusaburō as editor. The existence of this diary began to be known in the early nineteenth century.

yoru sariba dare ni kakarite nagusamamu
come night, who will it lean to for love and care?

This linking occurred on the fifteenth of the third month in 1499, and the aristocrat Sanjō-Nishi Sanetaka (1455–1537) recorded it in his diary. That day Sōchō and Sōgi, both towering masters in orthodox renga, had come to visit him with wine. In the ensuing game of renga, the participants were, apparently, trying to see who could come up with links the fastest. Sōgi's link was risqué, haikai, and therefore out of place, and probably neither he nor Socho expected their host to record such an exchange for pos terity. Sanetaka himself noted that this was the only consecutive set he remembered from that gathering. But both Sōchō and Sōgi also expounded on *haikai no renga* elsewhere. When occasion required, they were perfectly capable of rising to it.

The following pairings are found in the influential haikai anthology *Inu-Tsukuba Shū* (The Dog's Tsukuba Collection),[13] the compilation of which is attributed to Yamazaki Sōkan (d. 1539?):

kokoro no uchi no yasashisa wa iza
his gentle thoughts—no, I can't say that

fude-yui no sugigate ni miru kabazakura
a brush-maker admires a wild cherry as he passes by

❀ ❀ ❀

omou hodo koso kurawarenikeri
they sucked me to their satisfaction

---

13   The origin of renga was traditionally traced to an exchange in verse that is said to have occurred in a place called Tsukuba, a story told in Japan's oldest extant book, *Kojiki* (Record of Ancient Matters), compiled in 712. Accordingly, the first anthology of orthodox renga, compiled in 1357, was entitled *Tsukuba Shū* (Tsukuba Collection). The word *inu*, "dog," is deprecatory, at least for the Japanese, hence the title of this early haikai anthology. Some of the early anthologies of renga, including haikai, such as *Tsukuba Shū* and *Inu-Tsukuba Shū*, consist of selections of two-link sets such as the ones cited here and hokku.

yomosugara yabure kachō no uchi ni nete
I slept one whole night in a tattered mosquito net

❀ ❀ ❀

nigiri hosomete tsutsu to irebaya
squeezing it slender, I'll slip it in quickly

hachatsubo no kuchi no sebakini ō-bukuro
the tea bag's too large for the tea jar's small mouth

Bashō the renga poet started out in a similarly humorous vein, if not with such overtly crude humor. But he soon outgrew this approach. In his day the defining feature of haikai no renga became the rejection of poetic diction and the adoption of daily language. The obvious humor was shed—replaced by subtle allusions to literature and ordinary customs and practices. As Bashō sought a higher poetry, the question for him also became how to transcend the chosen diction itself.

And, while the general prosodic rules remained the same, the standard length of the sequence for haikai no renga was shortened from one hundred links to thirty-six. The sequence of thirty-six links is commonly called *kasen,* "poetic saints," in reference to the earlier custom of making a list of the thirty-six greatest poets.[14]

The Hokku and Salutation

Some of the general rules of renga composition are explained in the prefatory note to *A Farewell Gift for Sora.* The basic rule is disjunctive linking: any two consecutive parts or links (5–7–5/7–7 or 7–7/5–7–5) must make a coherent whole, but three may not. This means that the narrative flow shifts its direction with each new link.

In a sequence designed not to have any narrative coherence, it did not take long for the 5–7–5-syllable hokku, the opening part,

---

14   The best-known selection was made by Fujiwara no Kintō (966–1041).

to be given the task of commemorating the occasion—the requirement to refer to what was or should be observed at the time and place where the session was held. Because seasonal elements were predominant in Japanese poetic tradition, this requirement usually meant mentioning some aspect of nature that tradition deemed appropriate for the season. This tradition is preserved in most haiku written today.

The commemorative nature of the hokku also brought in the element of *aisatsu*, "salutation" or, for want of a better word, what could be called "salutatoriness." Since the hokku is the most prominent part of the sequence, its composition ought to be accorded, it was decided, to the most adept in the group, who was often a "master" or someone of comparable status and just as often the guest of honor. That being the case, the person assigned the hokku would compliment some aspect of the occasion in his piece.

Unlike the seasonal specifiers, kigo or kidai, salutatory elements can be indirect and convoluted. Let us look at one of the more direct examples from *Narrow Road to the Interior*. Toward the end of the account, there occurs a description of the Mogami, which is famed as one of Japan's three fastest flowing rivers.

The Mogami River rises in Michinoku, originating as it does in Yamagata. It has terrifyingly dangerous spots such as Go Stones and Falcon. It flows north of Mount Itajiki and in the end enters the sea at Sakata. From left and right, mountains close in, and the boat rides down through foliage. The so-called *inafune* must be the boats loaded with rice that ply the waters here. The White-thread Falls splash down through rifts in green leaves. The Sennin Hall stands right at the water's edge. In the brimming water our boat looks precarious.

Samidare o atsumete hayashi Mogami-gawa
Gathering the May rains and swift, the Mogami River

The original version of this hokku read:

Samidare o atsumete suzushi Mogami-gawa
Gathering May rains and cool, the Mogami River

The difference between *hayashi*, "swift," and *suzushi*, "cool," is telling. A sequence of thirty-six parts with this hokku as the opener was composed in the house of Takano Ichi'ei, an official in charge of the river (though some say he was in the business of boat-rental), during a two-day period, from the twenty-ninth to the thirtieth of the fifth month, which corresponds to mid-July by the solar calendar. The day must have been hot and humid, so Bashō complimented the host by saying that on account of the river that he oversaw, the scenery felt *cool*—an important seasonal notion for summer. However, when he later incorporated the hokku into his narrative as an independent piece, Bashō decided to shed the more personally complimentary "cool" and replaced it with "swift," which he probably felt was more satisfactory as a faithful description of the river.

Ichi'ei, in any case, responded to this compliment by composing a self-deprecatory 7–7-syllable:

> *kishi ni hotaru o tsunagu funagui*
> on the bank, boat poles moor fireflies

This is self-deprecatory because, in effect, Ichi'ei is saying that the place he is in charge of is not a thriving port with a great many boats but a place frequented only by fireflies.

The relationship between the hokku and the second unit in a renga sequence, called *wakiku* or *waki*, is rooted in the traditional mode of Japanese greeting. As Hattori Tohō (1657–1730) quotes Bashō as saying, *Waki, teishu no ku o ieru tokoro, sunawachi aisatsu nari*, "The waki is something the host makes, and it has to be salutatory" to the guest. Tohō adds that Bashō told his students, *Setsugetsuka no koto nomi iitaru ku nite mo aisatsu no kokoro nari*, "One conveys the sense of salutation even in a verse unit describing only the snow, the moon, or the flower." The snow, the moon, and the flower—the cherry flower—are the most representative symbols of seasonal change.

In a larger sense, too, the salutatory elements were important, for if a kidai or kigo was meant to laud the spirit of the season, the aisatsu was intended to praise the spirit of the place. This is why Bashō stressed the importance of taking into account the *kurai*, "rank" or "status," of a given place when composing a hokku on it. One might say that in the example just cited Bashō's aisatsu moved from a human being to a river when he changed "cool" to "swift."

The Independence Versus the Integration of the Hokku

The revision of the piece on the Mogami River brings us to the question of the independence of the hokku as a verse form. From the outset, the foremost requirement of the hokku was that it work as an independent verse. Technically, the hokku was not completely cut off from the renga until the literary reformer Masaoka Shiki (1867–1902) termed the renga "nonliterature" and urged the writing of hokku as independent literary pieces. But already by Bashō's day, writing hokku without the slightest thought of having them open renga sequences had become far more common than not. Bashō himself, who has left us about a thousand hokku, is known to have used only one out of eight of them to start a renga. Of his fifty-odd hokku incorporated in *Oku no Hosomichi*, only nine were used for the original purpose of beginning a sequence, even though renga sessions were an indispensable part of his travels and he took part in at least thirty.

The problem with the hokku when treated as an independent literary piece was the same as that of its grandparent, the tanka: it was too short. To make up for this deficiency, hokku, except where the circumstance of composition was apparent to those concerned, often came with certain explanations—just as tanka had. Indeed, with tanka, there was, from early on, a genre known as *uta monogatari*, "poetic tales"—collections of episodes each explaining the circumstance of the composition of a specific tanka. You might even say that the famed *Genji Monogatari* (The Tale of Genji) is a form of uta monogatari, interspersed as it is with eight hundred tanka. Tanka were also incorporated into other forms of narrative, such as memoirs and diaries.

In writing *Oku no Hosomichi*, other travel accounts, and episodic essays, lengthy and brief, Bashō was following this tradition. In travel accounts in particular, he wanted to emulate, he said, Ki no Tsurayuki (d. 945) and the Nun Abutsu (d. 1283).[15] Tsurayuki wrote *Tosa Nikki* (Tosa Diary), a description of his travels from Tosa (today's Kōchi), where he completed his assignment as governor at the end of 934, to his house in Kyoto, where he arrived in the second month of the following year. Abutsu wrote *Izayoi Nikki* (The Diary of the Sixteenth-Day Moon), an account of her travels from Kyoto to Kamakura, in 1279, to bring a lawsuit against a relative and of her four-year stay in that seat of military government. Both *michi no nikki*, "diaries on the road," as Bashō called them, are interwoven with poems—*Tosa Nikki* with 57 tanka and *Izayoi Nikki* with 116, ending with a *chōka*, "long poem," praying for victory in the lawsuit.

Let us look at a typical paragraph from each account. In *Tosa Nikki*, which is written in the persona of a woman,[16] as the old governor prepares to leave, the new one invites him and his entourage to his mansion for a farewell banquet, on the twenty-fifth of the twelfth month. The banquet turns rowdy and continues on to the next day.

> On the twenty-sixth. Still at the governor's mansion, the host made a good deal of racket, giving gifts even to the attendants. He loudly recited Chinese poems. As for poems in Japanese, the host, the guests, and everyone else made them for one another. I wouldn't dare write the Chinese poems here.[17] As for Japanese poems, the host, the governor, recited:

---

15   In *Oi no Kobumi*, Bashō names a third poet, Kamo no Chōmei (?1155–1216), apparently in the belief that he was the author of *Kaidō Ki* and *Tōkan Kikō*, but both travel accounts were composed a few decades after Chōmei's death and their author or authors remain unknown.

16   Diaries in those days were kept by men writing in Chinese. Tsurayuki, writing this diarylike account in Japanese, apparently felt it desirable to pretend to be a woman.

17   The writer, being a woman, is supposed to be ignorant of Chinese.

Miyako idete kimi ni awan to koshi mono o koshi kai mo naku
wakarenuru kana
Leaving the City I have come all the way to meet you,
but all in vain for we must part

To this, the governor who was going back said:

Shirotae no namiji o tōku yukikaite ware ni nibeki wa tare
naranakuni[18]
Having crossed the white-cloth wave-path from the dis-
tance, you, who else, will be like me

There were pieces by other people, but none of them
were clever enough.

In *Izayoi Nikki* there also occurs a scene where the writer pre-
pares to leave. Abutsu refers to her own sons by their court titles:
Tamesuke, then sixteen years old, as *jijū*, "gentleman-in-waiting,"
and Tamemori, then fourteen, as *taifu*, "gentleman of the fifth
rank." Her husband, the poet Fujiwara no Tame'ie, had died four
years earlier, in 1275.

> Even when I am not negligent, our garden and the hedges
> tend to turn wild, but now—so thinking, I couldn't help
> looking around. Also, I was unable to soothe those who
> loved me as they wet their sleeves with tears. I was par-
> ticularly pained by the Gentleman-in-Waiting and the
> Gentleman of the Fifth Rank who seemed to have utterly
> succumbed to grief, though I used various words. Then I
> happened to look in my bedroom and saw my husband's
> pillow left unchanged as in the past, which made me even
> sadder. So I scribbled near it:

> *Todomeoku furuki makura no chiri o dani ware tachisaraba tare ka*
> *harawan*

---

18   That is, in the end you, too, will complete your assignment and, like me, return to
      the capital.

Even the dust on the old pillow I have kept, who will
brush it off after I leave?

Haibun, an Attempt at a New Poetic Prose

"All the writings" following these travel accounts had not been
able to improve on them, Bashō said, his own not excepted, he
being "shallow in wisdom and short of talent." Indeed, his four
travel accounts preceding *Oku no Hosomichi,* including *Oi no
Kobumi,* are unsatisfactory, each failing to strike a balance be-
tween prose and poetry or lacking in narrative flow.

Bashō spent more than four years composing *Oku no Hoso-
michi,* revising and polishing it, showing it to his trusted friends
for suggestions. Finally, in the early summer of 1694, a few
months before his death, he decided he had chiseled it into an
acceptable form. His care and effort were amply rewarded. From
the beginning it won high praise. Pithy, brief, varied, and well-
cadenced, it moves with a certain inevitability. The strategically
placed hokku (and occasional tanka) help this movement along,
just as overlooks and scenic spots on the highway help the traveler
along by providing moments for rest. In design and execution,
Oku no Hosomichi far excelled the works Bashō wanted to emulate,
Tosa Nikki and *Izayoi Nikki.* And it remains unexcelled.

It was apparently while composing and revising this account
that Bashō came upon the notion of *haibun*[19] or haikai prose. A
style of writing influenced by the Japanese adoption of poeticized
Chinese prose, haibun was, in Bashō's mind, something to con-
trast with *gabun* or elegant prose in classical Japanese. At times
accentuated by verse, it was to be imbued with a modest, de-
tached, transcendental sense, the sense that even the rustic and
vulgar have poetry in them. Haibun, in short, is heightened prose
shorn of sentimentality. In view of their polish, Baudelaire would
have gladly called Bashō's best haibun—and *Oku no Hosomichi* is
the very best among them—prose poems.

---

19   In his extant letters Bashō used this word for the first time in a letter to Mukai Kyorai
(1651–1704), which he is believed to have written in the eighth month of 1690.

The Title

Oku no Hosomichi, the title Bashō gave his account, may derive from the short path with the same name that he and Sora visited in Sendai during the trip—in reality, a new uta-makura created to promote local prestige and tourism *(Narrow Road,* p. 73). But the scholar Shiraishi Teizō is convincing when he argues that Bashō probably had in mind *Tsuta no Hosomichi,* "Narrow Path of Ivy," an older uta-makura deriving from *Ise Monogatari* (Tales of Ise), and gave the ninth-century name a haikai twist.[20] Accepting this view, we might say that Bashō rejected the courtly literary ideal of elegance and replaced it with his own ideal in a more ordinary but "deeper" realm.

The Translation

Oku no Hosomichi has been translated into English by various hands, with different English renditions of the title as well. Let us see how some have dealt with the opening sentences:

Tsukihi wa hakutai no kakaku ni shite yukikau toshi mo mata tabibito nari. Fune no ue ni shōgai o ukabe uma no kuchi o toraete oi o mukauru mono wa, hibi tabi ni shite tabi o sumika to su.

Days and months are travellers of eternity. So are the years that pass by. Those who steer a boat across the sea, or drive a horse over the earth, till they succumb to the weight of years, spend every minute of their lives travelling.
                    NOBUYUKI YUASA, *The Narrow Road to the Deep North and Other Travel Sketches,* 1966

Moon & sun are passing figures of countless generations, and years coming or going wanderers too. Drifting life

---

20   Sakamoto Gen and Shiraishi Teizō, *Oku no Hosomichi* (Kodansha, 1975), pp. 165–66.

away on a boat or meeting age leading a horse by the
mouth, each day is a journey and the journey itself home.

CID CORMAN AND KAMAIKE SUSUMU, *Back Roads to
Far Towns*, 1968

The months and days are the wayfarers of the centuries,
and as yet another year comes around, it, too, turns travel-
er. Sailors whose lives float away as they labor on boats,
horsemen who encounter old age as they draw the horse
around once more by the bit, they also spend their days in
travel and make their home in wayfaring.

EARL MINER, *The Narrow Road Through the
Provinces* in *Japanese Poetic Diaries*, 1969

The passing days and months are eternal travellers in
time. The years that come and go are travellers too. Life
itself is a journey; and as for those who spend their days
upon the waters in ships and those who grow old leading
horses, their very home is the open road.

DOROTHY BRITTON, *A Haiku Journey: Bashō's
Narrow Road to a Far Province*, 1980 (revised)

The sun and the moon are eternal voyagers; the years
that come and go are travelers too. For those whose lives
float away on boats, for those who greet old age with
hands clasping the lead ropes of horses, travel is life,
travel is home.

HELEN CRAIG MCCULLOUGH, *Narrow Road of the
Interior* in *Classical Japanese Prose: An Anthology*,
1990

The moon and sun are eternal travelers. Even the years
wander on. A lifetime adrift in a boat, or in old age lead-
ing a tired horse into the years, every day is a journey,
and the journey itself is home.

SAM HAMILL, *Narrow Road to the Interior*, 1991

When there are so many translations, why try another?

My reply is that with translations, as with most other things, the preference, in large measure, is a reflection of taste. No doubt each of these renditions has its own partisans. I can name one among my poet friends who favors the experimental Corman and Kamaike version, which, in my view, is unnecessarily awkward, though it may not be apparent from the opening sentences. I can name another who commends the version by my ever-accommodating friend Professor Earl Miner, which strikes me as often too explanatory. Similarly different assessments exist for the other translations, I am sure.

In my rendition I have tried to stay as close to the original as possible. This approach extends to the hokku, which, though it consists of three distinct units of 5, 7, and 5 syllables, is normally written in one line and regarded as a one-line poem. I have also provided detailed notes. The extent of the annotations might make Bashō appear derivative, but as I have pointed out elsewhere (and as everyone knows), the "cult of originality" is something new to our literary experience. A rich fabric of reference—in good hands, such as Shakespeare's, Eliot's, or Bashō's—is an incomparable resource and a source of wonderment.

Finally, I have translated the opening portions of all the renga for which Bashō wrote the hokku during the journey, as well as a complete renga sequence in which Bashō took part. With these features, *Bashō's Narrow Road* is, I trust, the first translation of *Oku no Hosomichi* that stresses the renga aspect of Bashō's literary activity in his exploration of the Interior. It should also enable the reader to ascertain the oft-made observation that this travel account is structured like a thirty-six-part renga.

Narrow Road
to the Interior

BASHŌ'S ROUTE,
WITH MAJOR STOPPING PLACES

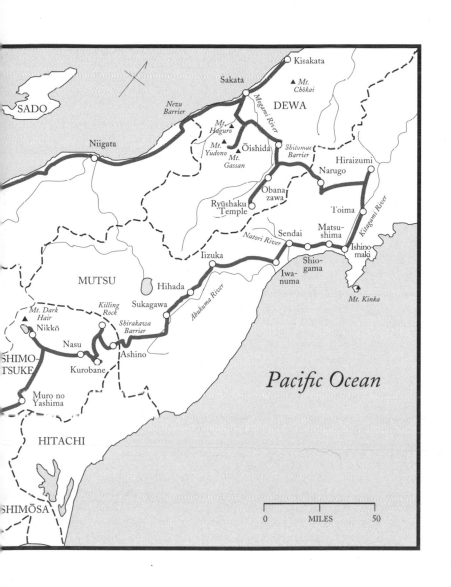

Pacific Ocean

Kisakata

Sakata

▲ Mt. Chōkai

Nezu Barrier

DEWA

Mogami River

SADO

Mt. Haguro ▲

Niigata

Mt. Yudono ▲

Mt. Gassan

Ōishida

Shitomae Barrier

Hiraizumi

Narugo

Obana zawa

Ryūshaku Temple

Toima

Matsu shima

Kitagami River

Sendai

Natori River

Ishino maki

Iizuka

Shio gama

Iwa numa

MUTSU

Hihada

Abukuma River

Mt. Kinka

Mt. Dark Hair ▲

Killing Rock

Sukagawa

Nikkō

Shirakawa Barrier

Nasu

Ashino

SHIMO-TSUKE

Kurobane

Muro no Yashima

HITACHI

SHIMŌSA

0   MILES   50

1 Alludes to the preface to "Holding a Banquet in the Peach and Pear Garden on a Spring Night" by Li Po (701–62) where the poet says: "Heaven and earth are the inn for all things, the light and shadow the traveler of a hundred generations. Accordingly, this floating life is just like a dream." Haikai poets liked these striking images and referred to them often.

2 Bashō probably had in mind Japanese poets such as Saigyō (1118–89) and Sōgi (1421–1502) and Chinese poets such as Li Po and Tu Fu (712–70), who all died while traveling.

3 Fukagawa, in Edo, is where Sugino Sampū (1647–1732), a wealthy merchant who sold live fish to the Tokugawa shogunate, gave a house to Bashō. To call that house "a dilapidated hut" or "grass hut," as Bashō does here, was probably a form of poetic license. The "old pond" in Bashō's famous hokku, *Furuike ya kawazu tobikomu mizu no oto,* "An old pond: a frog jumps into the water the sound," may have been one of the manmade ponds there in which live fish were kept.

4 Shirakawa no Seki: an uta-makura. See the Introduction, p. 19–20.

5 *Sozoro-gami.* May be a deity concocted during Bashō's time.

6 An uta-makura. Literally "pine islands," Matsushima is a bay in Miyagi, dotted with more than 260 islets. For Bashō's travel plans for the year, see endnote 1.

7 The kigo, "seasonal word," is *hina,* "dolls," because here it refers to what is today called *Hina-matsuri,* the Dolls' Festival. Also known as the Peach Festival or Girls' Day, it was held on the third of the third month, by the lunar calendar the last month of spring. (Today it is held on March 3.) In one collection this hokku comes with a preface that says: "I gave the hut where I lived for some time to someone I knew. He had a wife, daughters, and grandchildren."

8 The renga sequence consisting of a hundred links, called *hyakuin,* was, for compositional purposes, divided into nine sections: the first and last sections, each consisting of eight links, and seven sections in between, each consisting of twelve links. Bashō may have composed a hundred-part sequence with his friends to commemorate his departure from his house in preparation for a long trek and left a sheet with the first eight links, or *omote hakku,* written on it hung on a post. The sequence, if it was composed, does not survive.

NARROW ROAD
TO THE INTERIOR

THE MONTHS AND DAYS ARE WAYFARERS OF A HUN-dred generations, and the years that come and go are also travelers.[1] Those who float all their lives on a boat or reach their old age leading a horse by the bit make travel out of each day and inhabit travel. Many in the past also died while traveling.[2] In which year it was I do not recall, but I, too, began to be lured by the wind like a fragmentary cloud and have since been unable to resist wanderlust, roaming out to the seashores. Last fall, I swept aside old cobwebs in my dilapidated hut in Fukagawa,[3] and soon the year came to a close; as spring began and haze rose in the sky, I longed to walk beyond Shirakawa Barrier[4] and, possessed and deranged by the distracting deity[5] and enticed by the guardian deity of the road, I was unable to concentrate on anything. In the end I mended the rips in my pants, replaced hat strings, and, the moment I gave a moxa treatment to my kneecaps, I thought of the moon over Matsushima.[6] I gave my living quarters to someone and moved into Sampū's villa:

Kusa no to mo sumi-kawaru yo zo hina no ie
In my grass hut the residents change: now a dolls' house[7]

I left the first eight links hung on a post of my hut.[8]

9 By the solar calendar, the sixteenth of May. Bashō had planned to leave earlier, but the year was unusually cold, and he had to postpone the departure.

10 In the *Hahakigi* (Broom Tree) chapter of *The Tale of Genji*, as Genji leaves Utsusemi, "Cicada Shell," old Iyonosuke's young wife to whom he has forcibly made love during a restless night, there occurs the following description: "Even though the moon at dawn loses much of its light, it was clearly visible, and the daybreak was all the more affecting as a result. The appearance of the sky, which has no intention one way or the other, could seem elegant or frightening, depending on the mood of the person who sees it." Bashō also may have had in mind several passages in the Suma chapter of the *Tale*.

11 In the tenth month of the second year of Nin'an (1167), Saigyō visited Kamo Shrine before going on a pilgrimage to Shikoku. Forty-nine at the time, he felt that he might not have another chance to see his beloved shrine and composed a tanka: *Kashikomaru shide ni namida no kakaru kana mata itsuka wa to omou kokoro ni,* "Awestruck my tears fall on *shide* adornments as I wonder when again, deeply moved" (his personal collection *Sanka Shū,* no. 1095). *Shide* refers to the strings made of tree bark or strips of paper attached to the decorative rope called *shimenawa* and other things found in a shrine. The nō play *Morihisa* has a similar phrase in a similar setting.

12 "Three thousand *li*" is a standard Chinese-style hyperbole. However, one Chinese *li* is about 600 yards while one Japanese *li* is about 4,000 yards. So, if Bashō was using the Japanese measure, the actual distance he and his companion Sora traversed would be 500 *li*, but if he was using the Chinese measure, it would be 3,300 *li*.

13 Alludes to the third and fourth lines of "A Spring View," a poem by Tu Fu: "Touched by the times, I shed tears on the flowers; / resenting the separation, I am startled by the birds." The kigo of this hokku is *yuku haru,* "departing spring," which denotes the last phase of that season.

14 The year 1689. It was the 500th anniversary of Saigyō's death. "It must be" is an attempt to recreate the original circumlocution, *niya.*

15 "Interior State": the region consisting of the five provinces north of Nakoso and Shirakawa Barriers on the Pacific side, i.e., Iwaki, Iwashiro, Rikuzen, Rikuchū, and Mutsu. Today these provinces correspond to the four prefectures of Fukushima, Miyagi, Iwate, and Aomori.

16 *Goten,* "the sky of Wu," is a traditional metaphor for a remote, alien land.

O N THE TWENTY-SEVENTH OF THE THIRD MONTH,[9] the daybreak sky was suffused with haze; even though the moon at dawn loses much of its light,[10] the peak of Fuji was faintly visible, and I was uncertain when again[11] I might see the flowering treetops of Ueno and Yanaka. My close friends, who had been gathered since the previous evening, sent me off in a boat. When we climbed out of the boat at a place called Senju, I was depressed by the thought of the three thousand *li* that lay ahead[12] and shed tears at a parting in this illusory world.

Yuku haru ya tori naki uo no me wa namida
Departing spring: birds cry and, in the eyes of fish, tears[13]

This was the first time I used my travel writing implements, and I was still reluctant to venture farther. My friends lined up along the road, apparently to keep watching us as long as they could see us.

T HIS YEAR, THE SECOND YEAR OF GENROKU IT MUST be,[14] I casually thought of making a pilgrimage over a long road to Ōshū[15] and, even while realizing that I could end up regretting my hair turning white under the sky of Wu,[16] I gambled on the slim, uncertain chance of return-

Setting off.

17   *Kamiko.* Made of layers of paper, it was initially monastic wear but was later adopted for ordinary use, even becoming a fashionable item to wear in the pleasure quarters during Bashō's days. It was also a metaphor for poverty or staying outside the establishment.

18   Unlined summer robes made of cotton. Originally *yu-katabira,* "unlined robe for bathing."

19   Often, when someone like Bashō set out on an extended journey, a situation the Japanese call *arigata-meiwaku,* or "no thanks but thanks," developed. Since Bashō fully expected this account to be read by all concerned, he might have meant this as a gentle admonition. See endnote 2.

20   An uta-makura identified as Ōmiwa Shrine in present-day Tochigi City; its origins are obscure. See endnote 3.

21   Sengen Shrine, in present-day Fujinomiya City, Shizuoka. An uta-makura.

22   Sora here refers to a mythological tale that appears both in the *Kojiki* (Record of Ancient Matters) and the *Nihon Shoki* (History of Japan). Though *muro* means "chamber," the connection of the name Muro no Yashima to the mythological tale is tenuous at best. See endnote 4.

23   Other than Sanekata's tanka cited in endnote 3, there are poems such as a tanka on spring by Minamoto no Toshiyori (1055–1129), in *Senzai Shū* (no. 7): *Kemuri ka to Muro no Yashima o mishi hodo ni yagate mo sora no kasuminuru kana,* "Even as I wondered if it was smoke from Muro no Yashima, the sky has become suffused with haze."

24   Identified as *Chatoessus punctatus,* a species of herring. See endnote 5.

25   Where Tokugawa Ieyasu (1542–1616), the founder of the Tokugawa shogunate, is entombed.

ing alive from a place of which I had heard but hadn't seen with my own eyes. And the day we left, we managed to reach the station called Sōka. The things that I had hung over my thin-boned shoulders tormented me first. Although I had left with practically nothing, there were things like a paper-garment[17] to keep me from night's cold, a *yukata*,[18] rainwear, and ink and brushes, in addition to which were the farewell gifts I was unable to decline. I was unable to discard them, either, and had to resign myself to their becoming a burden on the road.[19]

W E PAID OUR RESPECTS TO MURO NO YASHIMA.[20] Sora, my companion on the road, said: "The deity here is called Princess-to-make-trees-bloom and is also enshrined on Fuji.[21] This is called Muro no Yashima because she shut herself up in a doorless chamber and vowed to burn herself, but in the midst of that act gave birth to Prince-fire-out.[22] It is also because of this that it is customary to mention smoke in a poem about this place."[23] Again, local history has it that catching the fish called *konoshiro*[24] is banned.

O N THE THIRTIETH WE STAYED AT THE FOOT OF Mount Nikkō.[25] The inn proprietor said, "My name is Buddha Gozaemon. Because my principle is to be

26   An oxymoronic compliment based on paradox.

27   "Strong will and rugged simplicity approach ultimate humanity" (Confucian *Analects*, XIII). Ezra Pound, who was fascinated by individual Chinese characters, translated the sentence: "The firm-edge, the persistent, the tree-like, those who hold in their speech, come near to full manhood" (*Confucius*, New Directions, 1969, p. 253).

28   Mount Nikkō.

29   In imitation of *Futarasen*, the Pure Land. The word *futara* was originally *fudaraku*, which derives from the Sanskrit *potalaka*, "where the Bodhisattva Avalokiteśvara manifests herself." The two Chinese characters applied to *futara* can also be read *nikō*, "two disasters." Legend has it that a storm used to arise twice a year from the cave northeast of this mountain.

30   Also known as Kōbō Daishi, "The Great Promulgator of the Law" (774–835). He changed the name to pacify the deity thought to be responsible for the twice-a-year storm. However, the original temple, Kegon, was founded by Shōdō (737–817). The confusion is said to have occurred because *Seirei Shū*, a collection of Kūkai's prose and verse in Chinese, has a tribute to Shōdō for successfully establishing a religious base there (*Seirei Shū*, section 11).

31   The kigo is *aoba wakaba*, "green leaves young leaves," which indicates the season is early summer. Sora recorded the initial draft of this hokku: *Ana tōto ko no shita yami mo hi no hikari*, "Oh, so holy: even in the dark under trees the light of the sun." This version is more unsubtly complimentary to Nikkō and, by extension, to Ieyasu, but apparently Bashō composed it while at Muro no Yashima.

honest in everything, people call me that. Please feel complete-
ly relaxed on your grass pillow and have a good rest." Wonder-
ing what kind of Buddha manifested himself in this world of
mud and dust to help someone like me, who resembled a Bud-
dhist mendicant or a pilgrim, I observed the proprietor's
behavior with some care and found him to be simply unwise
and undiscriminating,[26] a man of honesty incarnate. It was like
strong will and blunt simplicity approaching ultimate humani-
ty.[27] His innate clarity of mind should be highly valued.

O N THE FIRST DAY OF THE FOURTH MONTH, WE PAID
our respects to The Mountain.[28] In ancient times
the name of this mountain used to be written to read *Futara-
san* (Mount Two Disasters),[29] but when the Great Teacher
Kūkai[30] founded the temple, he changed it to *Nikkō* (Sun-
light). He must have foreseen the future a thousand years
ahead: today the light from this place illuminates the entire
heaven, its beneficence fills the whole land, and the easeful
home for all four classes of people is peaceful. Awestruck, I
was barely able to take up my brush:

Ara tōto aoba wakaba no hi no hikari
Look, so holy: green leaves young leaves in the light of
 the sun[31]

32   Kurokami-yama: an uta-makura. Minamoto no Yorimasa (1104–80) has a tanka on winter in *Shin-Go-Shūi Shū* (no. 563): *Mi no ue ni kakaramu koto zo tōkaran Kurokami-yama ni fureru shirayuki,* "It will happen to me not far in the future: on Mount Dark Hair falls white snow."

33   *Koromogae* is the custom of changing clothes for the summer and for the winter. By the lunar calendar, the fourth month was the first month of summer.

34   *Bashō,* from which the poet derived his name. In a haibun in praise of this plant, Bashō wrote: "Its leaf is wide enough to cover a koto. At times, blown down midway, it pains you like the phoenix's broken tail or, like a torn green fan, it sorrows in the wind. From time to time its flowers bloom but they are not florid, and though its stalk is thick, it is never axed. Comparable to 'useless trees in the mountain,' it is noble in character. Monk Huai-su ran his brush on it, while Chang Heng-chu, looking at its new leaves, gained strength for greater learning. I do neither; simply idling beneath its leaves, I admire the way they tear easily in wind and rain."

35   Bashō wrote a haibun on Sora; see endnote 6.

36   An uta-makura.

37   Actually, Bashō composed the piece.

MOUNT DARK HAIR[32] HAD HAZE AROUND IT, ITS snow still white.

Sori-sutete Kurokami-yama ni koromogae[33]　　　　—SORA
Shaving off the dark hair mountain and clothes changed

Sora is from the Kawai family; his common name is Sōgorō. With our eaves side by side under the lower leaves of plantain,[34] he helps me in the labor of acquiring firewood and water.[35] This time he was delighted to share with me the views of Matsushima and Kisakata;[36] at the same time, to console me for the hardship of traveling, on the day he left for this journey he shaved his hair, changed his appearance to that of one in an ink-dyed robe, and revised the characters of his name from *sōgo* (all five) to *sōgo* (religious enlightenment). This is why he came up with the piece on Mount Dark Hair.[37] The two-character word *koromogae* sounds powerful.

We climbed the mountain for more than two thousand yards and came to a waterfall. Flying down a hundred feet from the top of a rocky cavern, it drops into an azure pool surrounded with a thousand rocks. I've heard it said that since you can put yourself in the cave and look at the water-fall from behind, it is called the Back-view Waterfall.

On the road near Nasu.

38   One training program for the summer required a Buddhist monk to confine himself in a room for ninety days, beginning on the sixteenth of the fourth month, to concentrate on copying and reciting sutras.

39   The castle town of the domain governed by the daimyo Ōzeki.

40   Sora noted that the inn there was so foul that they had to force themselves on the village head.

41   Bashō apparently had in mind the following passage from the nō play *Nishikigi:* "Today we have spent the whole day lost on these narrow paths. Where is the Nishiki-zuka? May that man cutting grass on the hill over there be kind enough to tell us clearly which is the path for human beings!"

42   The original phrasing is highly compressed: "Why don't you let this horse go, at whichever place he stops?"

43   *Kasane* means "layers," while *nadeshiko,* the plant known as pink, is often associated with a girl because of its literal meaning, "caressed child." This prompted Bashō to add a somewhat hyperbolic honorific prefix, *yae,* "eight-layer," "eightfold," which really means "double," as in *yae-zakura,* "double-petal cherry." The plant named *yae-nadeshiko* by itself does not exist. This hokku is also Bashō's composition, not Sora's.

Shibaraku wa taki ni komoru ya ge no hajime[38]
Confining ourselves in a waterfall a while in early summer

BECAUSE WE HAD AN ACQUAINTANCE AT A PLACE called Kurobane,[39] in Nasu, we decided to take a straight path there through the wild field that opened up before us. Aiming at a village in the distance, we kept going, but it started to rain and dusk fell. We borrowed space at a farmer's house for the night[40] and as soon as the day broke we resumed our walk through the field. There was a horse being pastured. We pleaded with a man who was cutting grass,[41] and the man, though a rustic, knew what compassion was, and was gracious enough to rent us the horse, saying: "I wonder what to do. You see, this field has paths crisscrossing it, and first-time travelers tend to take the wrong paths. I'm concerned about that. Take this horse, let him carry you as far as he goes, and, when he stops, let him go."[42]

Two small children followed us, running after the horse. One of them was a small girl and her name was Kasane. It was an unfamiliar name but elegant:

Kasane towa yae-nadeshiko no na narubeshi[43]   —SORA
Kasane must be another name for "eightfold" pink

44 *Nanigashi,* here given as "so-and-so," is a conventional way of referring to someone. Jōbōji's personal name was Takakatsu, and he had haikai pen names such as Tōsetsu (Peach Snow) and Shūa (Autumn Crow). Twenty-eight at the time, he was in charge of the administration of the fiefdom in the absence of its lord-president, Ōzeki Masutsune, who was in Edo.

45 Kakobata Toyoaki, twenty-seven at the time. Tōsui (Peach Green), or Suitō (Green Peach), was his haikai pen name. He and his friends were the first people with whom Bashō and Sora had a renga session during this journey. Bashō's hokku, *Magusa ou hito o shiori no natsuno kana,* "Someone carrying hay my marker through this summer field," was followed by Tōsui's waki, *aoki ichigo o kobosu shii no ha,* "green strawberries sprinkled on pasania leaves." This typical exchange between guest of honor and host was followed by Sora's *murasame ni ichi no kariya o fukitorite,* "a shower blowing over a fair booth."

46 *Inuoumono* or *inuoi,* a game in which men on horseback compete in shooting a dog with blunted arrowheads.

47 According to the legend given in the nō play *Sesshōseki* and others, in China a golden fox with nine tails transformed herself to marry a king, then crossed over to Japan, and became Retired Emperor Toba's favorite mistress, Lady Tamamo. When her true identity was exposed, she fled to Nasu where she was shot to death. Her wraith then turned itself into the *sesshōseki,* "the killing rock." The same legend has it that "dog chasing" originated when warriors started practicing horseback shooting in order to kill the demonic fox.

48 During the battle of Yashima, in early 1185, the Taira forces, retreating to the sea, challenged the Minamoto forces to shoot a fan a woman held up at the tip of a pole on a swaying boat. Nasu no Yoichi, ordered by the commanding general Minamoto no Yoshitsune (1159–89) to accept the challenge, successfully shot down the fan. As recounted in *Heike Monogatari* (The Tale of the Heike), his prayer before shooting may be translated: "Hachiman the Great Bodhisattva I revere, Enlightener of my Province, Avatar of Nikkō at Utsunomiya, Great Gracious Deity of Yuzen, Nasu, allow me to hit the fan right in the middle! Should I fail in this, I would cut the string, break the bow, and kill myself to save myself from the embarrassment of facing any man again." Hachiman is the guardian deity of the samurai, especially of the Minamoto clan, and Hachiman shrines exist throughout Japan.

49 The original for "rough training" is *shugen,* the exceedingly rough religious training required among the followers of Shugen-dō. Typically it requires a follower to retreat into the mountains to go through self-imposed hardships so that he may experience a divine state of mind.

50 To make walking difficult, the wooden clogs used by the followers of Shugen-dō are said to have one support, not the normal two. Bashō and Sora are about to enter the Ōu region, hence *kadode,* "depart." The first draft of this hokku was: *Natsuyama ya kadodeni ogamu taka-ashida,* "Summer hills: at departure we pray to the tall clogs."

In time we reached the village. We tied a sum to the seat of the saddle and sent the horse back.

W E VISITED JŌBŌJI SO-AND-SO,[44] THE CASTLE deputy of Kurobane, in his house. He was delighted with our unexpected visit, and we went on talking throughout days and nights. His brother, named Tō-sui,[45] came to visit us mornings and evenings whenever he could, taking us to his own house as well. We were also invited by their relatives as the days went by.

One day we wandered out into the suburbs, took a look at a place where dog chasing[46] used to be practiced, and waded into the Bear-bamboo of Nasu to pay a visit to the old grave of Lady Tamamo.[47] From there we went to Hachiman Shrine. Because we had heard it was this shrine that Yoichi invoked when he prayed, "Above all, my tribal deity, the right Hachiman, of my province," before shooting through the target fan,[48] our veneration was especially deep. As dusk fell, we returned to Tōsui's house.

There is a temple for rough training called Kōmyō.[49] Invited there, we paid our respects to the Ascetic Hall.

Natsuyama ni ashida o ogamu kadode kana[50]
Summer hills: we pray to the clogs as we depart

51   The twenty-first abbot of Kompon Temple, with whom Bashō studied Zen. When Kashima Shrine took away half of the land owned by his temple, he sued the shrine. After nine years he won the suit and resigned his abbotship. He was born a year before Bashō and died in 1715, at age seventy-two. See endnote 7.

52   This tanka expresses Butchō's regrets that he has to live in a hut, however small it may be, to take shelter from the rain. A true Buddhist is not supposed to have any fixed abode.

53   The fourth month, the first month of summer.

54   According to Sora's note, these were mainly prominent rocks and stands of plum and bamboo.

55   The original for the gate is *sammon,* "mountain gate," so called from the belief that a temple ought to be built on a wooded mountain.

56   A Zen monk of Southern Sung (1238–95). He is known for having confined himself in a cave to meditate for fifteen years. A frame with the inscription "Death Barrier" hung at the entrance.

57   Possibly a monk from the Liang dynasty who built a hut on a single rock and engaged in Zen discourse all day, every day.

I N THIS PROVINCE, FAR INSIDE UNGAN TEMPLE, THERE IS a place in the mountains where Monk Butchō[51] used to live. He had written to me some time back that he had scribbled on the rock there with pine charcoal:

Tateyoko no go-shaku ni taranu kusa no io
   musubu mo kuyashi ame nakariseba[52]
A grass hut less than five by five—I regret living
   even in it: if only there were no rainfalls!

To see the place, I went to Ungan Temple using a walking stick. People invited others, many of them young, and there was a good deal of gaiety on the way; before I knew it, we had reached the foothills. The mountain appeared deep; the path along the valley was long, with pine and cedar black, water oozing and dripping from the moss, and even though it was Deutzia Month,[53] the air still felt cold. Where the Ten Views[54] were exhausted, we crossed a bridge and entered the gate.[55]

So, where is it?—wondering, we climbed the mountain from the other side and found on a boulder a small hut leaning on a cave. It was like looking at the "death barrier" of Zen Master Miao[56] or the rock room of Monk Fa-yün.[57]

58   *Kitsutsuki,* woodpecker, is also called *teratsutsuki,* "temple-pecker." According to *Gempei Seisui Ki* (Record of the Rise and Decline of the Minamoto and Taira), the name derives from the legend that Monobe no Moriya (d. 587), who wanted to eliminate Buddhism, turned into a bird after he was killed and pecked at and damaged the high parts of Buddhist temples. The suggestion of the hokku is that even a bird that pecks at a temple has left this hut alone. Bashō had to use the weak phrase, "summer trees," to clarify the season because the woodpecker is a kigo for autumn.

59   Sesshōseki. Cf. note 47. Described as a pyroxene andesite rock seven feet square and four feet high. Apparently right on top of a volcanic vein, it exudes sulfur hydrogen, carbon dioxide, and other noxious gasses from the soil around it.

60   The kigo of this hokku is "cuckoo." In English literature the cuckoo suffers from a poor reputation and negative associations; in Japanese literature the bird represents summer—just as the cherry blossoms represent spring, the moon autumn, and snow winter—and anyone with poetic sensibility was expected to look forward to hearing its calls. However, exactly what Bashō meant to express by this hokku is subject to debate, with some commentators suggesting that he wanted to contrast his shabby-looking self with a gallant mounted warrior of the past.

61   The nō play *Sesshōseki* is based on the legend that Zen Monk Gen'nō (1329–1400) shattered the rock with his staff, turning its evil soul into a buddha.

62   Saigyō has a tanka: *Michinobe ni shimizu nagaruru yanagi kage shibashi tote koso tachidomaritsure,* "In willow shade on the roadside where clear water flowed, I stopped, saying, 'Just for a while.'" This poem became famous because of the nō play, *Yugyō-yanagi,* which is based on it.

63   Ashino Suketoshi (1637–92). His haikai pen name was Tōsui (Peach Drunk). He was evidently given the ceremonial court rank at the Imperial Ministry of Popular Affairs, for *kohō* is the Chinese name of that ministry. To call the lord of a fiefdom *gunshu,* "chief of the county," was also a Chinese affectation.

Kitsutsuki mo io wa yaburazu natsu kodachi[58]
Even woodpeckers don't tear at the hut in summer trees

I left this impromptu hokku on a post.

FROM THERE WE WENT TO THE KILLING ROCK.[59] Courtesy of the castle deputy, we went on horseback. The man who was leading my horse asked, "Would you write a poem card for me, sir?" I was touched by his elegant turn of mind:

No o yoko ni uma hikimuke yo hototogisu[60]
Turn the horse round across the field, cuckoo

The Killing Rock is near a foothill where hot water bubbles up. Its poisonous power has not died out;[61] so many bees and butterflies lie dead that the sand around it is scarcely visible.

The willow tree with "clear water flowing"[62] was in the village of Ashino, by a paddy ridge. Kohō so-and-so,[63] the chief of this county, had written to me from time to time to say, "I'd like to show you the willow," so I had wondered in what kind of place it would be. Today I was able to stop in the shade of this willow.

64   Alludes to a tanka on parting by Taira no Kanemori (d. 990), *Tayori araba ikade miyako e tsugeyaran kyō Shirakawa no Seki wa koen to,* "If I had some means, I'd like to send word to the City that today I have passed Shirakawa Barrier." The poem is included in *Shūi Shū* (no. 339).

65   The other two of the "three barriers in Ōu" are Nezu Barrier, which was in Dewa, and Nakoso Barrier, in Hitachi.

66   Alludes to a famous tanka by Priest Nōin (b. 988): *Miyako o ba kasumi to tomoni tachishikado akikaze zo fuku Shirakawa no Seki,* "Though I left the City with haze rising, autumn wind blows at Shirakawa Barrier." *Miyako,* "the City," is Kyoto; *kasumi,* "haze," indicates spring. Also see the Introduction, p. 19. In Nōin's personal collection, this poem has a headnote, "In the second year of Manju [1025] I had to go to Michinokuni suddenly. When I lodged at Shirakawa Barrier [I made the following poem]." Yet some of the later commentators said that Nōin made this poem without going to Shirakawa Barrier; they did this to suggest that a person of poetic sensibility can make good poems about places without actually seeing them.

67   The warrior-poet Minamoto no Yorimasa has left a tanka, *Miyako niwa mada aoba nite mishika domo momiji chiri-shiku Shirakawa no Seki,* "Though I saw the City still in green leaves, fallen crimson leaves carpet Shirakawa Barrier." The poem is included in *Senzai Shū* (no. 365).

68   Fujiwara no Kiyosuke (1104–77). His book on poetics, *Fukuro no Sōshi,* has this passage (Section 65): "When a man by the name of Takeda Taifu Kuniyuki went to Mutsu, he changed his costume and smoothed his hair with water on the day he passed Shirakawa Barrier. Someone asked, 'Why?' In reply, he said, 'How can I pass in ordinary clothes a place of which Lay Priest Kosobe [Nōin] said, 'Autumn wind blows at Shirakawa Barrier'?'"

Ta ichimai uete tachisaru yanagi kana
One paddy planted I walk away from the willow tree

AFTER DAYS PASSED WITH US FEELING UNCERTAIN, WE reached Shirakawa Barrier and finally began to feel we were on the road. Now I understood what was meant by "I'd like to send word to the City."[64] Above all, this being one of the Three Barriers,[65] people with sensitive minds have taken note of it. With the autumn wind in my ear[66] and red leaves in my mind's eye,[67] I was still moved by the green leaves on the treetops. Deutzia flowers making white brocade, wild roses vying in bloom, I felt as if I were passing through the barrier in snow. I'm told that Kiyosuke[68] has written that in the old days, people used to adjust their headgear and straighten their garments.

U no hana o kazashi ni seki no haregi kana —SORA
Deutzia flowers donned, for the barrier a special costume

IN TIME, WE PASSED THE BARRIER, WENT ALONG, AND crossed the Abukuma River. High to our left rose the peak of Aizu, and to our right were the villages of Iwaki, Sōma, and Miharu; behind us was a mountain range as if to

Living in the shade of a chestnut tree.

69   Kagenuma.

70   The original for "station" is *eki*, a place which by law dating from the seventh century was required to maintain basic amenities for travelers, such as horses, boats, and laborers.

71   Sagara Izaemon (1638–1715), then the chief of Sukagawa Station. Once a resident of Edo, he knew Bashō.

72   See endnote 8.

73   Yanai Yasaburō (dates unknown), whose Buddhist name was Kashin and whose haikai pen name was Rissai (Chestnut Food).

74   Alludes to Saigyō's tanka: *Yama fukami iwa ni shitadaru mizu tomen katsugatsu otsuru tochi hirou hodo,* "Mountain deep, I'll collect the water dripping from rocks, for now picking fallen horse chestnuts."

partition Hitachi and Shimotsuke. We passed a place called Mirror Marsh,[69] but today, the sky leaden, it did not reflect things well.

At Sukagawa Station[70] we visited a person named Tōkyū,[71] who put us up for four or five days. The first thing he asked was, "How did you pass Shirakawa Barrier?" I said, "These long travels have been painful, and I was exhausted body and soul. At the same time my heart was entranced by the land-scape and I was so profoundly moved thinking of things of the past that I did not come up with anything brilliant. Still, I could not possibly pass the place without a piece:

Fūryū no hajime ya Oku no taueuta
The start of poetry: a rice-planting song in the Interior."

This was followed by the second, third links, and we ended up completing three sequences.[72]

Near this station there was a monk who had removed himself from this world, choosing to live in the shade of a large chestnut tree.[73] I thought of his quiet existence as reminiscent of "the mountain where horse chestnuts were picked"[74] and wrote out the following. The words were:

75 A great fund-raising monk (668–749) who helped build Tōdai Temple and fund a number of social welfare programs.

76 According to Sora's note, the original version read *Kakurega ya me ni tatanu hana o noki no kuri,* "Hideaway: inconspicuous flowers on the chestnut near the eaves." As a compliment of the hermitage, it is more direct than the revised version. With this original, a thirty-six-link renga was completed. Rissai followed it with *mare ni hotaru no tomaru tsuyukusa,* "at times a firefly stops at a dayflower," in which the firefly is Bashō and the dayflower, a humble wildflower, Rissai. Tōkyū followed it with *kirikuzusu yama no i no na wa arifurete,* "gouged, the mountain well has gotten commonplace." Here the mountain well is a famous one used as a uta-makura.

77 Though by Bashō's time *katsumi* was generally thought to refer to blue flags, a common iris, the true identity of the plant so famous in poetry remained undecided. Among the more famous tanka on the plant is this anonymous one on love: *Michinoku no Asaka no Numa no hana-katsumi katsu miru hito ni koi ya wataran,* which, giving *katsumi* as "flags," may be translated: "Flowering flags in Asaka Swamp of Michinoku: a lover as infrequently seen will she have to be?" It is included in *Kokin Shū* (no. 677). Suffering the fate of things famous for centuries, the Asaka Swamp itself was by then "a disgusting ditch in a paddy," as Tōkyū sadly noted.

78 Kurozuka, "black mound," is an uta-makura. It is the legendary abode of an ancient she-devil who entrapped travelers, sucked their blood, and devoured their flesh. There is a nō play called *Kurozuka,* also known as *Adachigahara.*

79 Shinobu-moji-zuri-no-ishi: an uta-makura. Shinobu, here a place name, also means "hare's-foot fern" and "think of (someone, the past)." Originally, *moji* was part of the word *mojiru,* "draw crooked or convoluted lines," but later it came to mean "letters, figures," creating the belief that you could reproduce those letters by rubbing a cloth placed over the stone with the sap of green leaves, as well as the belief that you could see the face of your lover by rubbing the stone with the sap of wheat. According to one report, the stone measured twelve by seven feet on top and was less than two feet high on one side and more than six feet high on the other. See endnote 9.

The character for "chestnut" combines "west" and "tree";
since it suggests the Pure Land to the West, Bodhisattva
Gyōgi[75] used this tree all his life, I am told, to make his
walking sticks and the pillars of his house:

Yo no hito no mitsukenu hana ya noki no kuri[76]
People hardly note its flowers: the chestnut near the eaves

ABOUT FIVE *LI* FROM TŌKYŪ'S HOUSE, OFF FROM
Hihada Station, was Mount Asaka. It was close to
the road. There were many swamps around. Because it was
not far from the time for harvesting *katsumi*,[77] I asked peo-
ple, "Which plant is the flowering *katsumi*?" but there was
not a person who knew. As we visited swamps, asked people,
and walked about mumbling, "*Katsumi, katsumi*," the sun
came down to the rim of hills. We turned right at Two
Pines, took a look at the Cave Abode of Kurozuka,[78] and
lodged in Fukushima.

THE FOLLOWING DAY, WE WENT TO SHINOBU VILLAGE
looking for the Stone for Rubbing Shinobu Fig-
ures.[79] In a foothills village far away, the stone lay half buried
in the ground. A boy from the village came by and told us:
"Long ago, this stone was on top of the mountain, but
passersby would trample upon the wheat going to test the

The two wives.

80 Rice planting is still going on. Whatever the story about the stone may be, the hands of the people planting seedlings in the paddies recall the ancient technique of rubbing-dyeing.

81 In this and some of the passages that follow, the thematic figure, though mentioned only once, is the military commander Minamoto no Yoshitsune. In 1180, when he joined his brother Yoritomo in the war against the rival Taira clan, his protector Fujiwara no Hidehira (d. 1187) provided him with two warrior brothers, Satō Tsugunobu (1158–85) and Tadanobu (1161–86). Both men proved good soldiers: Tsugunobu died fighting to shield Yoshitsune; Tadanobu committed suicide when overwhelmed in battle after Yoritomo started a campaign to kill Yoshitsune following the war. To console their mother, their widows are said to have put on armor to pretend they were Tsugunobu and Tadanobu returning in triumph. Shōji was their father.

82 "To wet one's sleeves" is a conventional way of saying "to weep."

83 When Yang-hu, an exceptionally virtuous governor during China's Chin dynasty, died, people built a commemorative stele for him. Because everyone who saw it shed tears, a poet named it "the Tear-shedding Stele."

84 Benkei (d. 1189) is a legendary warrior monk who remained steadfastly loyal to Yoshitsune; he died fighting when Hidehira's son, Yasuhira (d. 1189), going against his father's will, attacked Yoshitsune at Yoritomo's instigation. See the Introduction, p. 20. In one of his letters the Jesuit Luis Frois (1532–97) called Benkei "the Hercules of Japan." The "casket" here refers to a sizable box containing a variety of paraphernalia that was carried on the back.

stone. People here hated it and pushed the stone down into
this valley. So it lies here, its face down." A likely story, or
was it?

Sanae toru temoto ya mukashi Shinobu-zuri[80]
The hands taking seedlings recall the ancient rubbing

W̲E CROSSED THE RIVER AT TSUKINOWA FERRY AND
came out at a station called Senoue. The site
where Satō Shōji's mansion used to be was located about one
and a half *li* toward the left, close to the mountain.[81] We heard
that it was at Sabano, in Iizuka Village. We asked for direc-
tions as we went along until we reached a place called
Maruyama. It was Shōji's old castle. A place below there was
where the main gate used to be, someone told us, and we shed
tears. Also, an old temple nearby retained the family's stone
steles. Among them the one about the two wives was the first
to touch me deeply. Women though they were, they have left
such a reputation of gallantry, I marveled, and wet my
sleeves.[82] You do not have to look far to find a Tear-shedding
Stele.[83]

When we went in the temple and asked for tea, we
learned that among its treasures were Yoshitsune's sword
and Benkei's casket.[84]

85 Refers to Tango: "One of the 5 popular feasts *(go-sekku)*, celebrated on the fifth day of the fifth month. It is the festival for boys. Each family raises a pole upon which flutter large carps made of paper or cloth, and intended to signify that as that fish ascends the strongest rapids, so also the child will surmount all obstacles in his path to fortune"—according to the description given in E. Papinot's *Historical and Geographical Dictionary of Japan* (1910). In reality, the carp is a rather sluggish, bottom-feeding fish.

86 Bashō is believed to have suffered from chololithiasis, which can cause a great deal of pain when the body is not kept warm. However, since Sora did not leave any special notation on this night, the second day of the fifth month, some conjecture that Bashō may have fictionalized this passage.

87 A poetically prescribed way of referring to a summer night.

88 The same phrase appears in the Confucian *Analects*, IX, but there Confucius is expressing a wish not to die on the road.

89 The original expression, *michi shō'ō ni funde,* is interpreted in opposite ways: "to walk with powerful steps" and "to totter like a wounded warrior on a battlefield." Those who take the former interpretation see the expression linked to the words with masculine associations that follow, Date and Ōkido (the order in which the words appear in the original). Date, the name of the daimyo of the fiefdom, is especially known for the one-eyed Masamune (1567–1636), a ferocious warlord; the name also had become a metaphor for dandyism and ostentation because of the colorful attire favored by men of the clan. Ōkido, a place name, means "great wooden door," the main gate to a castle.

Oi mo tachi mo satsuki ni kazare kaminobori[85]
Display both casket and sword in May with paper carps

This happened on the first day of the fifth month.

THAT NIGHT WE STAYED IN IIZUKA. THERE WAS A HOT spring, so we took a bath, then sought a lodging place. It turned out to be a disturbingly poor house with straw mats laid on the earth floor. Because there was not even a lamp, we made our bed by the light from the fire pit and lay down. At night thunder rumbled and rain fell without interruption. There were leaks where we lay, and, bitten by fleas and mosquitoes, we were unable to sleep. Even my chronic illness[86] revived, and I almost fainted. As the sky of the short night[87] finally lightened, we resumed our travels. With the remnants of the night still with me, I rented a horse and we went out to Ko'ori Station. We still had such a great distance ahead of us that the kind of illness I had made me feel uncertain, but by reminding myself that this was a journey, a pilgrimage to remote corners, that I had resolved to abandon the secular world, resigned as I was to the transience of all things, and die on the road,[88] and that all this was a fate ordained by Heaven, I regained my strength a little and trod on the road as I pleased,[89] and we went beyond Ōkido, Date.

Taga Castle Stone Marker

90 Fujiwara no Sanetaka (d. 998). Because of his ill-tempered behavior at the court, Emperor Ichijō (980–1011) appointed him governor of Mutsu so that he might "check out some poetic places." Though he was in his governor's post for three years before his death, legend has it that he fell off his horse and died on his way to his post because he didn't bother to dismount when he passed by a shrine for the guardian deity of the road.

91 Minowa.

92 Kasajima.

93 When he visited Sanetaka's grave, Saigyō made a poem: *Kuchimosenu sono na bakari o todomeokite kareno no susuki katami nizo miru,* "Only his name retained without decay, I regard the pampas grass in this withered field as his keepsake."

94 The Pine of Takekuma (Takekuma no Matsu) and the Natori River are both uta-makura. According to *Ōgi Shō,* a treatise on poetics by Fujiwara no Kiyosuke (1104–77), Fujiwara no Motomaro, while governor of Mutsu, planted a pine tree in front of his mansion. The tree was subsequently replanted twice, but Fujiwara no Takayoshi cut it down to make bridge pilings. The book says Minamoto no Mitsunaka (a.k.a. Manjū; d. 997) and Tachibana no Michisada also replanted the tree, but it does not mention the Natori River.

95 Nōin's poem on a miscellaneous subject in *Go-Shūi Shū* (no. 1042), which comes with a headnote, "I again went down to Michinokuni and during this later trip there was no more of the Pine of Takekuma, so I made this poem": *Takekuma no matsu wa kono tabi ato mo nashi chitose o hete ya ware wa kitsuran,* "The Pine of Takekuma now has left no trace, I having arrived here after a thousand years have passed."

A S WE PASSED ABUMIZURI AND SHIROISHI CASTLES and entered Kasajima County, we asked a person the whereabouts of the grave of Captain First Secretary Sanetaka[90] and were told: "The foothill villages you can see from here in the distance, to the right, are called Raincoat Ring[91] and Hat Isle[92] and there we still have the shrine for the guardian deity of the road and 'the keepsake pampas grass.'"[93] On account of the May rains of the past several days, the road was terrible, and I was tired besides, so we walked ahead, seeing the villages in the distance. I decided that both names, Raincoat Ring and Hat Isle, were appropriate for the May rains:

Kasajima wa izuko satsuki no nukari michi
Where is Hat Isle?—this road so mired in May

W E STAYED IN IWANUMA. The Pine of Takekuma was truly eye-opening. Its trunk forked out into two at the ground, and you knew it hadn't lost its old appearance. First I thought of Priest Nōin. Perhaps because the gentleman who had earlier come down here as governor of Mutsu is said to have cut it down and used it as bridge pilings at the Natori River,[94] he made a poem saying "the pine now has left no trace."[95] I'd heard that

96 Kusakabe Kyohaku (d. 1696), a merchant who studied haikai with Bashō. "Someone named" is a circumlocution.

97 The suggestion of this hokku is that by the time Bashō arrives in Iwanuma, it will be the time for late-blooming cherries. One interpretation stresses, however, that it may even be too late for the late-blooming cherries to be enjoyed, so the cherries must make sure to show the visitor Bashō the green pine tree.

98 Alludes to a tanka by Tachibana no Suemichi (d. 1060) in *Go-Shūi Shū* (no. 1041), which has a headnote, "I went down to Michinokuni with Norimitsu Ason and made a poem on the Pine of Takekuma": *Takekuma no matsu wa futaki o miyako-bito ikaga to toeba miki to kotaen,* "The Takekuma Pine has two trunks; should a City person ask, 'How is it?,' I'd reply, 'I've seen it.'" Suemichi's poem relies on a pun: *miki,* "I've seen it," also means "three trunks." Aside from the numerical playfulness, Bashō's hokku also uses a pun: *matsu,* which means both "pine tree" and "to wait for." In an earlier version of this hokku, the first five syllables appear to have been *chiri-usenu,* "[the cherry blossoms have] completely fallen away." Bashō evidently sent this hokku to Kyohaku in his letter. Kyohaku used it as the opening piece for his anthology, *Shiki Sen-ku* (A Thousand Hokku for the Four Seasons), published in 1689.

99 On the fourth day of the fifth month, blue flags were hung from the eaves to repell evil spirits.

100 Kitanoya Kaemon (dates unknown), a ranking student of the haikai poet Ōyodo Michikaze (1639–1707). In addition to carving for wood-block printers, he ran a bookstore specializing in haikai books.

101 That is, uta-makura. At the time both the government of the Sendai fiefdom, under the direction of Date Tsunamura, and its citizens were trying to reestablish or create poetic places in Sendai—apparently to promote the tourist industry.

102 Tamada and Yokono are uta-makura so designated by Michikaze and friends. Minamoto no Toshiyori has a poem: *Tori-tsunage Tamada Yokono no hanare uma Tsutsuji no Oka ni asemi sakunari,* "Capture and tether the horses let loose in Tamada and Yokono: *asemi* bloom on Azalea Hill." For *asemi,* see note 104.

103 Tsutsuji-ga-Oka: an uta-makura.

104 Also called *asemi (Pieris japonica).* "Shrub 2–4 m. high . . . inflorescence pendulous, densely many-flowered, minutely puberulent; flowers white, nodding, short-pedicellate," according to *Flora of Japan.* Miner calls it "the pony grass," Britton "the lily of the valley," Hamill "andromeda flowers." The juice from *asebi* leaves used to be used as an insecticide and for treating a skin disease. It was thought that these leaves would intoxicate horses, hence the three Chinese characters applied to the name, "horse-intoxicating tree," and hence Toshiyori's poem cited in note 102.

105 Kinoshita: an uta-makura.

from time to time people had cut the tree down and planted a new one, but for a thousand years to this day it has retained its shape; a felicitous pine tree it is indeed.

> Because someone named Kyohaku[96] had given me a
> farewell gift: *Takekuma no matsu mise mōse oso-zakura*,
> "Show him the Takekuma Pine, late-blooming cherry"[97]

Sakura yori matsu wa futaki o mitsuki goshi[98]
Three months since the cherry: the two-trunk pine

WE CROSSED THE NATORI RIVER AND ENTERED Sendai. It was the day blue flags were hung.[99] We sought out an inn and stayed for several days.

Here, there was a wood-block carver named Kaemon.[100] Hearing that he had some interest in poetry, I became acquainted with him. "I have looked into some of the famous places whose locations have become uncertain over the years,"[101] he said, and guided us around one whole day. The bush clover in Miyagi Plain grew luxuriantly, making me wonder how it might look in the fall. Tamada, Yokono,[102] then on to Azalea Hill[103] where *asebi*[104] were in bloom. We went into a pine forest where no sunlight came in, and were told the place was called Under-the-tree.[105] It must be because the dew was dense in the past as well that

106   Alludes to an anonymous tanka "from the East" in *Kokin Shū* (no. 1091): *Mi-saburai mi-kasa to mōse Miyagino no ki no shita tsuyu wa ame ni masareri,* "Servant, tell your lord, 'Umbrella, sir!' for the dew under the trees in Miyagino is worse than the rain."

107   Bhaiṣajyaguru, the Buddha of medicine.

108   *Tenjin* is a general term for "heavenly deity"; it also denotes Sugawara no Michizane (845–903), who after his death was revered as a deity of learning.

109   An uta-makura—in the earlier days the number one uta-makura in Mutsu. Literally "salt vat" or "salt oven," Shiogama was known for salt production, which entailed back-breaking labor, as well as for its haunting beauty. With a headnote, "While I was aggrieved about the transience of this world, I saw a painting of famous places in Michinokuni," Murasaki Shikibu (fl. 1000) made a tanka on sorrow: *Mishi hito no keburi to narishi yūbe yori na zo mutsumajiki Shiogama no Ura,* "Since the evening someone close turned into smoke I've felt intimate with the name, Shiogama Bay." Alluding to the smoke that was said to rise constantly from the vats boiling sea water, the smoke here refers metaphorically to cremation. The poem is included in *Shin-Kokin Shū* (no. 820).

110   According to Sora's diary, that day, the seventh of the fifth month, Kaemon, along with a man named Jimbei, visited Bashō and Sora in the evening and gave them a bag of dried rice, along with the sandals. In return, Bashō gave each visitor a card with a hokku and a painting, which he probably made on the spot. The following morning Kaemon came to visit again to give them a sheaf of dry seaweed.

111   The original for "someone demented" is *shiremono,* and that for "elegant pursuits" is *fūryū.* In haikai and other such pursuits, to be described as "demented" or "eccentric" was a compliment.

112   Tofu no Suge: an uta-makura designated by Date Tsunamura. A farmer was given a special annual stipend to grow the sedge needed for making the "poetic mats."

113   Oku no Hosomichi: an uta-makura created by Michikaze and others. According to Sora, the path was within the premises of a peasant's house and along a paddy ridge, on one side of which the sedge in question was planted. See the Introduction, p. 33.

114   At the time, Date Tsunamura.

115   Tsubo no Ishibumi, which is said to have been found when Tsunamura ordered an archeological dig on the site where Taga Castle, mentioned immediately afterward, was believed to have stood. Taga Castle was a stockade built during the Nara period (710–84) to fend off the Ezo people. See endnote 10.

someone made a poem saying, "Servant, Umbrella."[106] We
offered prayers at Yakushi[107] Hall and the holy shrine for Ten-
jin,[108] and the day came to an end. In addition, Kaemon drew
certain places of Matsushima and Shiogama[109] and gave the
drawing to us as a present. Furthermore, he gave us two pairs of
straw sandals with indigo-dyed thongs as a farewell gift.[110]
When it came to this, he truly revealed himself to be someone
demented by elegant pursuits.[111]

Ayame-gusa ashi ni musuban zōri no o
Blue flags will be tied to our feet above sandal thongs

A S WE WALKED ALONG, RELYING ON KAEMON'S DRAW-
ing, there was the "Ten-plait Sedge"[112] on the hill-
side of the Narrow Road to the Interior.[113] It is said that
even today, each year, ten-plait sedge mats are prepared and
presented to the governor of the province.[114]

Tsubo Stone Marker.[115]   It is in Taga Castle, in Ichikawa
Village.

Tsubo Stone Marker is perhaps a little over six feet high,
about three feet wide. The moss dug aside, the letters were
barely visible. It indicated the distances to the national bor-

116 The "nations" here included Pohai, the short-lived country northeast of Korea, facing the Japan Sea. It came into being in 713 and was destroyed by 926. This part of the inscription reads: "1,500 *li* from Kyoto, 120 *li* from Ezo, 412 *li* from Hitachi Province, 274 *li* from Shimotsuke Province, and 3,000 *li* from Pohai."

117 The era lasted from 724 to 729.

118 A tentative translation of *azechi*, a position charged with assessing governors' work and conduct, as well as popular sentiments in the provinces.

119 Also Azumabito, Azumando (d. 742). He took part in an expedition to subjugate the *Ebisu*, northern "barbarians," and put down the revolt of Fujiwara no Hirotsugu (d. 740).

120 The era lasted from 757 to 765.

121 A tentative translation of *setsudoshi*, an emergency position charged with overseeing the military affairs of a given region.

122 The original inscription repeats "Commander-in-Chief of the Pacification Headquarters." Bashō's copy includes omissions and errors.

123 Fujiwara no Nakamaro's son (d. 764). Nakamaro (706–64), who, on account of his political achievements, was given the honorary name of Emi no Oshikatsu, revolted and was put down. Asakari was killed along with him.

124 The Jinki era occurred during the reign of Emperor Shōmu, which lasted from 724 to 749, and the Tempyō Hōji during the reign of Emperor Jun'nin, which lasted from 758 to 764. By "this," Bashō apparently refers to the founding of the castle.

125 Alludes to a remark in Section 93 of *Tsurezuregusa*—rendered as "Essays in Idleness" by Donald Keene—of Yoshida Kenkō (1283–1350): "If we hate death, we should love life. The joy of being alive—why shouldn't we enjoy it every day?"

126 One of the six rivers bearing the name *tama* (jewel). Actually a rivulet between paddies. Tsunamura designated it as an uta-makura.

127 Oki no Ishi, the uta-makura created by Tsunamura for a tanka on love by Nijōin Sanuki (dates uncertain) in *Senzai Shū* (no. 760), which has a headnote, "I made a poem on 'Love Compared to a Stone'": *Waga sode wa shiohi ni mienu oki no ishi no hito koso shirane kawaku ma mo nashi*, "My sleeves are like the stone in the offing invisible with the tides out: unknown to anyone but no time to dry." Sanuki described a rock near the seashore, but the rock designated by Tsunamura for a uta-makura is in a pond. The poem is included in *Hyakunin Isshu* (One Hundred Poems by One Hundred Poets), a popular anthology initially compiled by Fujiwara no Teika (1162–1241).

128 Sue no Matsuyama: an uta-makura. Famous for an anonymous tanka "from the East" in *Kokin Shū* (no. 1093), *Kimi o okite atashi kokoro o waga motaba Sue no Matsuyama nami mo koenan*, "Should my heart turn fickle at your expense, waves would go over the Pine Hill of Sue," and the tanka by Kiyohara no Motosuke (908–90) in *Go-Shūi Shū* (no. 770), which alludes to it, *Chigirikina katami ni sode o shiboritsutsu Sue no Matsuyama nami kosaji towa*, "Did we not vow, wringing each other's sleeves, that 'waves would not go over the Pine Hill of Sue'?" The latter is included in *Hyakunin Isshu*.

129 The location of Sue no Matsuyama remained unidentified until Date Masamune renovated a Zen temple, which then received the name Masshōzan, the Sinified reading of Sue no Matsuyama.

ders in the four directions.[116] I read: "This castle was laid down, in the first year of Jinki,[117] by Inspector-General[118] and Commander-in-Chief of the Pacification Headquarters Lord Ōno Azumahito.[119] In the sixth year of Tempyō Hōji,[120] it was completed by Councilor, Subjugator[121]-of-the-Eastern-Sea-and-the-Eastern-Mountains, and ditto[122] Lord Emi no Asakari.[123] The first day of the twelfth month." This corresponds to the reign of Emperor Shōmu.[124]

There are a great number of poetic place names people have handed down to us as sung of in poems since long ago. However, as mountains collapse, rivers shift, and paths are renewed, stones are buried and hidden in the ground and trees age and are replaced by young ones, the passage of time and the changing world making me see, so far, only uncertain traces of them. But now, finally, here was an indubitable monument from a thousand years ago, which, right in front of my eyes, allowed me to contemplate the minds of ancient people. This was one virtue of pilgrimage, the joy of being alive.[125] I forgot the ordeals of travel and could not hold back the tears that flowed down.

FROM THERE WE VISITED TAMA RIVER OF NODA[126] AND Offshore Stone.[127] For Pine Hill of Sue,[128] they built a temple, calling it Masshōzan.[129] The spaces between

The blind monk plucking a biwa.

130   Phrases that occur toward the end of Po Chü-i's famous narrative poem, "Song of Everlasting Regret": "In heaven, I pray we'll turn into two birds with a single wing,/on earth, I pray we'll turn into a branch linking two trees." These images are metaphors for everlasting love.

131   An anonymous tanka "from the East" in *Kokin Shū* (no. 1088), *Michinoku wa izuku wa aredo Shiogama no Ura kogu fune no tsunade kanashimo,* "In Michinoku I can't say where, but in Shiogama Bay, a skiff rowing, pulled with a rope, is truly sad," and a tanka by Minamoto no Sanetomo (1192–1229) in *Shin-Chokusen Shū* (no. 525), which alludes to it, *Yononaka wa tsune ni mogamona nagisa kogu ama no obune no tsunade kanashimo,* "May the world be ever like this: a fisherman's skiff rowed along the shore, pulled with a rope, is truly sad." The latter is included in *Hyakunin Isshu.*

132   A four-stringed, lute-like musical instrument.

133   *Jōruri* is a form of dramatic recital accompanied by a musical instrument. *Oku-jōruri* refers to this form of recitation that developed in and around Sendai.

134   *The Tale of the Heike,* a military tale originally recited to the accompaniment of the biwa.

135   *Kōwaka-mai,* a simple dance performed with a recitation of a simple tale. It was popular among the warrior class during Japan's age of warring states.

136   Shiogama Shrine, the most important one in Ōshū. Shiogama became particularly famous after Minister of the Left Minamoto no Tōru (822–95) made an elaborate garden on Kyoto's Kamo riverbed in the form of a miniature replica of Shiogama Harbor and its surroundings (hence his later sobriquet, The Minister of the Left of the Riverbed). *Tales from Ise* has a tanka (Episode 81): *Shiogama ni itsuka kiniken asanagi ni tsurisuru fune wa koko ni yoranan,* "I seem to have come to Shiogama; boats fishing in the morning calm are sure to come by." Attributed to an old beggar who was moved to praise the garden, the poem says that the garden has such a striking resemblance to Shiogama that it will soon attract fishing boats.

137   Date Masamune.

the pine trees were all covered by graves. As I thought that all the pledges for "a single wing" and "a linked branch"[130] finally end up like this, my sadness increased. We then heard the vesper bell on Shiogama Bay. The May-rain sky cleared up a little and, under the faint evening moon, Magaki Isle was close by. Fishermen's boats rowed back, and as I heard the men dividing their catch, I was moved, recalling the heart of someone who had to say "pulled with a rope, truly sad."[131] That night, a blind monk plucked the biwa[132] to narrate something called Oku-jōruri.[133] It was not the *Heike*[134] or a *mai*,[135] but as he raised his rustic tune high, though he was quite noisy near my pillow, I couldn't help admiring him for not forgetting an old tradition in such a forsaken place.

EARLY IN THE MORNING WE PAID OUR RESPECTS TO the Deity of Shiogama.[136] A governor of the province[137] had revived the shrine. Its columns are thick, the rafters brilliantly painted, the stone steps built exceedingly high, and the morning sun made the crimson fence sparkle. It was admirable to think that the Divine Soul should manifest himself so conspicuously at one end of the road and in the borderland, part of the Way of our Nation though it may be.

In front of the Deity there was an old lantern. On the sur-

The Takadachi, Hiraizumi.

138   Fujiwara no Tadahira (1167–89). He tried to defend Yoshitsune in accordance with his father Hidehira's wishes; as a result, he was killed by his own brother, Yasuhira.

139   The year 1187.

140   Alludes to a statement of Han-yü (768–824): "One can easily be slandered, and one's reputation can suffer."

141   The second largest freshwater lake in China, famous for its scenery.

142   A lake in Chê-chiang Province famous for its beauty.

143   The Ch'ien-t'ang River, of Chê-chiang Province, is famous for the tidal disturbances at its estuary. Unlike those of most rivers, this estuary is much narrower than the body of the river leading to it. This feature, plus the great difference between high and low tides, causes a spectacular onrush upriver at the estuary when the tide flows in.

144   Japanese used to—some still do—carry a child piggyback.

145   Alludes to a line in a poem of Tu Fu called "Viewing Mountain Peaks": "Various peaks in a row resemble children, grandchildren."

face of its metal door was written: "Presented by Izumi no Saburō[138] in the Third Year of Bunji."[139] I could conjure up his face from five hundred years ago and was unaccountably enthralled. He was a brave, righteous soldier with filial dedication. His great reputation survives to this day, and there is not one who does not admire him. Truly, a man should cultivate the Way and stick to righteousness. "One's reputation can suffer,"[140] it is said.

It was already noon. We rented a boat and crossed to Matsushima. After about two *li*, we arrived on the shore of Ojima.

ALTHOUGH THIS HAS BEEN SAID A NUMBER OF TIMES, Matsushima is the most beautiful scenery in Japan and wouldn't embarrass itself alongside Lake Tung-t'ing[141] and Lake Hsi.[142] It allows the sea in at the southeast, with the bay inside three *li* across, brimming with the tides of Chê-chiang.[143] There are an inexhaustible number of islands, some steeply rising, pointing at heaven, some lying, prostrating themselves on the waves. Some are piled twice, heaped thrice, parted to the left, linked to the right. There are some that carry others on their backs,[144] some that hug others in their arms, as if loving their children, grandchildren.[145] The green of the pines comes in delicate shades,

146   The word translated as "ineffable" is *yōzen* (in Chinese, *yaojan*), which is interpreted variously to mean "disappointed," "dazed" (as in "he was dazed and had forgotten his kingdom there," in Burton Watson's translation of *Chuang Tzu,* Columbia University Press, 1968, p. 34), "suggestive," and "far away" (as in Li Po's poem, "Question and Answer in a Mountain": "Someone asks me why on earth I live in a dark-green mountain. / I do not respond, my heart naturally content. / Peach blossoms flow far away in a stream. / This is a different world, not of the human kind.").

147   In his poem, "Drinking on the Lake at the First Sign of Clearing Up After a Rain," Su Tung-p'o (1036–1101) compares Lake Hsi to Hsi-shih: "If I picked up Lake Hsi and compared it with Hsi-shih, / it should be like her in all aspects, made up lightly or heavily." Hsi-shih, the beloved queen of Wu King Fu-ch'a, during the Spring Autumn Period, is considered the most beautiful woman in Chinese history.

148   Ōyamatsumi, a deity in charge of mountains.

149   *Chihayaburu,* here translated as "rock-smashing," is a *makura-kotoba,* an epithet that modifies *kami,* "deity," and other words.

150   In *Go-Shūi Shū* Minamoto no Shigeyuki (d. 1000?) has a tanka on love (no. 827): *Matsushima ya Ojima no iso ni asariseshi ama no sode koso kaku wa nureshika,* "In Matsushima, fishermen working the Ojima shore had sleeves that were indeed as wet as these." These sleeves are wet with tears for unrequited love.

151   A monk (1582–1659) from Myōshin Temple, Kyoto. In 1636 Date Tadamune invited him to revive Zuigan Temple.

152   Another circumlocution. Actually the residence still stood there, named Hafujū-ken.

153   In the elegant setting of Matsushima, the cuckoo, though representative of summer, is inelegant to behold so ought to appear as a graceful crane. The pine tree and the crane are a traditional pictorial combination. The hokku may also be a twist on a tanka attributed to Monk Yūsei: *Mi ni zo shiru Mano no irie ni fuyu no kite chidori mo karu ya tsuru no kegoromo,* "I now feel it: winter having arrived in the Mano inlet, plovers must borrow cranes' feather cloth." The tanka is cited in *Sarumino Sagashi* (1829) as the poem to which Sora alludes.

154   I.e., giving up any attempt to make a poem. In his book on haikai poetics, *San Zōshi,* Hattori Tohō (1657–1730) quotes Bashō as saying, "When you face splendid scenery, you become too entranced to make a poem," adding, approvingly, "Our teacher did not make a poem in Matsushima. This is important." See endnote 11.

and their branches are blown bent by the salty winds as if they had created their crookedness by themselves.

Matsushima is ineffable,[146] made up like a beauty's face.[147] All this may have been the doing of the Great Mountain God[148] in the days of rock-smashing[149] deities. The Creator's heavenly handiwork—who can use his brush or exhaust words to his satisfaction?

The Ojima shore, connected to the mainland, is an isle jutting out into the sea.[150] There are things like the site where Zen Master Ungo's[151] detached residence used to be[152] and his Zen meditation rock. I also saw under pine trees a smattering of people who had renounced this world quietly living in a grass hut from which smoke rose from a fire of gleanings and pine cones. I did not know who they were, but I stopped by, feeling close to them. The moon shining on the sea gave a view different from that of daytime. We went back to the bay shore and sought an inn. It had a second floor with an open window, and as we lay in the midst of wind and cloud, I felt mysteriously exhilarated.

Matsushima ya tsuru ni mi o kare hototogisu[153]   —SORA
In Matsushima, borrow a crane's guise, cuckoo

Mouth shut,[154] I tried to sleep and could not. When we

155 Yamaguchi Sodō (1642–1716), a samurai who pursued various arts: the art of drinking tea, calligraphy, nō recitation, *kanshi* (verse in Chinese), and *waka* (verse in Japanese, as opposed to kanshi; most often it refers to tanka).

156 A kanshi—probably the one of four 7-character lines that may be translated: "In early summer Matsushima will be clear and profound, / the calls of cuckoos above the clouds not certain yet. / The view will cleanse your mind as with water, / I'm touched that the azure emerald will reflect in your eyes." This translation is based on my friend Kyoko Selden's interpretation. Sodō also gave Bashō a hokku, *Matsushima no matsukage ni futari haru shinan*, "In the pine shade of Matsushima the two of us shall die in spring," which alludes to Saigyō's tanka, *Negawaku wa hana no shita nite haru shinan sono kisaragi no mochizuki no koro*, "I pray to die under blossoms, in spring, in the second month, about the time of full moon."

157 A physician (dates unknown), who was also a distinguished tanka poet at the time.

158 See note 155, above.

159 Matsu ga Urashima: an uta-makura.

160 See the opening of this travel account and note 3.

161 Nakagawa Jokushi (dates unknown). He was a close associate of Ōishi Yoshio (1659–1703), the leader of forty-seven samurai famous for a vendetta.

162 Heishirō (dates unknown), whose Buddhist name was Hosshin, revived the temple as a Zen temple of the Rinzai sect at the invitation of Hōjō Tokiyori (1227–63). He went to China during the Sung dynasty (960–1279). So Bashō is in error here. The original temple was founded by the Great Teacher Jikaku (794–864), also known as Ennin, of the Tendai sect.

163 Actually, the renovation of the temple was carried out earlier, when Date Masamune was the lord of the fiefdom.

164 Kembutsu is a twelfth-century monk who is reputed to have recited sixty thousand scrolls of the *Lotus Sutra* during the twelve years he lived on Ojima. His contemporary Saigyō respected him so much that he went all the way to Matsushima to meet him again, hence the reference to "*that* holy man."

165 Aneha no Matsu: an uta-makura. *The Tale of Ise* (Episode 14) has a poem: *Kurihara no Aneha no Matsu no hito naraba Miyako no tsuto ni iza to iwamashi o*, "If the Aneha Pine at Kurihara were a woman, I'd say, 'Let's go,' to take her as a gift to the City." The episode has to do with a Kyoto man who went to Michinoku and slept with a rustic woman because she thought it would be wonderful to sleep with a city man. Afterward, her reaction was somewhat coarse, so he made this poem to suggest that if she were at least as elegant as the Aneha Pine, he would gladly take her to Kyoto.

166 O-dae no Hashi: an uta-makura. Fujiwara no Michimasa (992–1054) has a tanka in *Go-Shūi Shū* (no. 751): *Michinoku no O-dae no Hashi ya kore naramu fumimi fumazumi kokoro madowasu*. One of the poems he wrote about his illicit affair with the *saigū* or vestal of Ise Shrine, Tōshi (d. 1023), it relies on a pun, *fumimi*, "try to step on" and "see letters" and means both "This must be the Thong-breaking Bridge of Michinoku: I feel bewildered whether I'm stepping on it or not" and "... I am bewildered that I see and don't see her letters." The affair is described in *Tama no Muragiku* and *Yūshide* chapters of *Eiga Monogatari*, a history of the Heian court from Emperor Uda (867–931) to Emperor Horikawa (1079–1107).

parted at my old hut, Sodō[155] had made a poem[156] on Matsu-shima. Hara Anteki[157] had kindly presented me with a *waka*[158] on Bay Isle of Pines.[159] I opened my bag and made them my company for the night. There were also hokku by Sampū[160] and Jokushi.[161]

O N THE ELEVENTH WE PAID OUR RESPECTS TO ZUI-gan Temple. This temple was founded thirty-two abbots ago by Makabe no Heishirō, after he returned to Japan from T'ang, where he had gone upon taking Buddhist vows.[162] Later, through Zen Master Ungo's virtuous prosely-tizing, its seven halls and roof-tiles were rebuilt, and with its golden walls and decorative Buddhist articles aglitter, it turned into a great cathedral, the Buddhist paradise on earth.[163] I could not help wondering where that holy man Kembutsu's[164] temple was.

O N THE TWELFTH WE MEANT TO GO TO HIRAIZUMI, but because we had heard about the Aneha Pine[165] and the Thong-breaking Bridge,[166] we took a road seldom used by people but frequented by pheasants, rabbits, and woodcutters,[167] and pushed ahead, until we took the wrong road and ended up coming out in a port called Ishi-nomaki. Across the sea we saw Mount Kinka, of which a

167   In literary tradition woodcutters were regarded as a breed apart—à la noble savages.

168   In the fourth month of 749, an imperial proclamation was made that gold had been found in the Japanese soil. In response, Ōtomo no Yakamochi (716?–85) made a set of poems that ended with a tanka: *Sumeroki no Miyo sakaen to Azuma naru Michinoku yama ni kugane hanasaku,* "So His Majesty's generation may prosper, on a Michinoku mountain to the east, gold has bloomed." Kinka itself means "gold blossom."

169   Refers to the story in *Nihon Shoki* that the sixteenth emperor, Nintoku, climbed an observation tower and was satisfied to see smoke rising from many peasant houses, for it was a sign that the country was prospering. *Shin-Kokin Shū* opens its section on felicitations with a tanka attributed to the same emperor: *Takaki ya ni noborite mireba keburi tatsu tami no kamado wa nigiwainikeri,* "I climb a tower and look around and smoke rises: my people are busy with their ovens."

170   Sode no Watari: an uta-makura. Sagami (994?-after 1061) has a tanka on love in *Shin-Go-Shūi Shū* (no. 931): *Michinoku no Sode no Watari no namida-gawa kokoro no uchi ni nagarete zo sumu,* "At Sleeve Ferry, in Michinoku, the river of tears flowing in my heart grows limpid."

171   Obuchi no Maki: an uta-makura. An anonymous tanka on a miscellaneous subject in *Gosen Shū* (no. 1252), which has a headnote, "We don't know what the man at first thought of her, but seeing that she wouldn't open up to him, he said, 'I hadn't expected you to be as strange as this,' [so the woman made this poem]": *Michinoku no Obuchi no koma mo nogau niwa are koso masare natsuku mono kawa,* "Even the horses of Mottled Tails, in Michinoku, if pastured, will become wilder, no, not tame."

172   Mano no Kayahara: an uta-makura. The correct name of *kaya* here is miscanthus. In *Man'yō Shū* (no. 396), Kasa no Iratsume (dates unknown) has a poem: *Michinoku no Mano no Kayahara tōke domo omokage ni shite miyu to iu mono o,* "The Sedge Field of Mano, in Michinoku, may be far but you can see it as an image, they say." What is implied is: Why can't I see you even in my mind's eye? Because you don't love me. This is one of a set of three poems Kasa no Iratsume sent to Ōtomo no Yakamochi.

173   Matsushima and Hiraizumi.

174   Of the Ōshū Fujiwara dynasty—from Kiyohira (1056–1128), Motohira (dates uncertain), to Hidehira. After inciting Hidehira's son, Yasuhira, to kill his own brother Yoshitsune, Minamoto Yoritomo then killed Yasuhira, thereby quickly terminating the glorious days of the Fujiwara clan in the north.

175   An instance in which the metaphor used in a Chinese admonitory tale changed as a result of the bastardized pronunciations of two characters, *ch'ui* (cook) and *chui* (sleep, nap), both of which are pronounced *sui* in Japanese. In the tale an ambitious young man named Huang-liang (Kōryō in Japanese) borrows a porcelain pillow from a Taoist preacher and takes a nap in which he dreams in great detail of the rise and fall of his whole life. When he wakes up, the millet meal he had started cooking before falling asleep is not yet ready. Because of this tale, "a dream in a single cooking" became a metaphor for the vanity of life. At some point, Japanese also started saying "a dream in a single sleep." Akutagawa Ryūnosuke (1892–1927) gives a wry twist to this tale in his short story, *Kōryō-mu.*

176   This side of what is uncertain, though apparently Bashō was trying to suggest the vast tract of land Hidehira had at his disposal.

poem saying "gold has bloomed" was presented to His Majesty.[168] Several hundred freight ships gathered in the inlet, houses vied for the land, and smoke kept rising from the ovens.[169] Wondering how we ended up in a place like this, we tried to find lodging, but no one was willing to let us lodge. Finally we managed to spend the night in a poor small house, and as the day broke, we resumed wandering along an unknown road. We walked on a long riverbank, looking at Sleeve Ferry,[170] Meadow of Mottled Tails,[171] and the Sedge Field of Mano[172] in the distance. After lodging one night in a place called Toima, which was along an elongated marsh, we reached Hiraizumi. The distance between the two[173] was a little over twenty *li*, I think.

THE GLORY OF THE THREE GENERATIONS[174] LASTED only as long as a single nap.[175] The place where the main gate stood was one *li* this side.[176] Hidehira's site[177] had turned into paddies, with only Kinkeizan[178] retaining its shape. First, we went up to the Takadachi[179] and saw the Kitagami was a large river flowing from Nambu.[180] The Koromo River flows around Izumi Castle and below the Takadachi pours into the large river. The old site for Yasuhira and others was on the other side of Koromo Barrier,[181] with the Nambu side fortified for defense, it seemed, against

177 Where his residence used to be. Samurai mansions in those days were often fortified enough to serve as castles.

178 Literally, "gold chickens mountain." Hidehira made a rooster and a hen of gold and buried them in a Fuji-shaped mound in his garden as guardians of Hiraizumi.

179 "High Mansion," which Hidehira gave to Yoshitsune. Yoshitsune was attacked and killed there.

180 More exactly, the domain owned by the Nambu family.

181 Koromo no Seki: an uta-makura. Izumi Shikibu (b. ca. 970) has a tanka on separation in *Shika Shū* (no. 173), which has a headnote, "After I was forgotten by Michisada, I sent this poem to him when he prepared to go to Michinoku as governor": *Morotomo ni tatamashi mono o Michinoku no Koromo no Seki o yoso ni kiku kana,* "I surely would leave with you, but can only indifferently hear about Koromo Barrier, in Michinoku." Izumi was estranged from her husband, Tachibana no Michisada (dates unknown), after she had consecutive affairs with Princes Tametaka and Atsumichi. Her poem uses a pun, *tatsu,* "leave, depart" and "cut [cloth]." *Koromo* means "cloth, clothes."

182 The first two lines from "A Spring View," a poem by Tu Fu.

183 Masuo Kanefusa (dates unknown), an old, white-haired warrior who, after making sure that Yoshitsune and his wife were dead, set fire to the Takadachi mansion and died fighting. He originally served the family of Yoshitsune's wife. Minamoto no Toshiyori (1055–1129) has a tanka: *U no hana no mina shiraga tomo miyuru kana shizu ga kakine mo toshiyorinikeri,* "All the deutzia flowers look like white hair, the lowly man's hedges having grown old." Was Toshiyori punning on his own name, which means "aged," "to grow old"? Most likely.

184 According to Sora's note, the person in charge was away that day and the Sutra Hall was not opened for the visitors.

185 Actually, the hall contains the statues of Bodhisattva Mañjuśrī (Japanese: Monju Bosatsu), Udayana the Great King (Uten Dai'ō), and Sudhana-śreṣṭhi-dāraka (Zenzai Dōji). Some commentators say that Bashō might have meant to say "the sutras of the three generals," because the hall did contain some of the sutras donated by the three leaders of the Fujiwara dynasty, Kiyohira, Motohira, and Hidehira.

186 Kiyohira, Motohira, and Hidehira, all mummified. The mummies have been subjected to scientific analysis in recent decades.

187 Amitābha (Japanese: Amida Nyorai), Avalokiteśvara (Kanzeon Bosatsu), and Mahāsthāmaprāpta (Seishi Bosatsu).

188 So designated in Buddhism. They are gold, silver, emerald (lapis lazuli), glass (crystal), giant clam, coral, and agate, though the list differs by sect.

the Ezo. The most loyal among his loyal vassals were select-
ed and put up in this castle, but their fame lasted only for a
moment and turned into clumps of grass. "The country
destroyed, the mountains and rivers remain. In the castle it is
now spring and the grass has turned green."[182] Sitting on our
hats laid on the ground, we shed tears for a while:

Natsukusa ya tsuwamono-domo ga yume no ato
Summer grass: where the warriors used to dream

U no hana ni Kanefusa miyuru shiraga kana[183]   —SORA
In deutzia flowers I see Kanefusa's white hair

The two halls about which I had heard so much were
open.[184] The Sutra Hall retained the statues of the three
guardian kings,[185] and contained in the Light Hall were the
coffins of the three generations,[186] with three Bodhisattvas[187]
rising peacefully above them. If left alone the seven trea-
sures[188] would have scattered, the jeweled doors torn in the
wind, and the gilt columns decayed in frost and snow, the
whole thing turning into dilapidation and empty grass in no
time; but it was newly enclosed on the four sides, and a tiled
roof was built above it to shelter it from wind and rain. So for
a thousand years now it has remained as a commemoration:

At Shitomae Barrier.

189   Ogurosaki: an uta-makura. The northern bank of the Arao River. For a poem, see the next note.

190   Mizu no Ojima: an uta-makura. A rock in the river. *Kokin Shū* has an anonymous poem among those "from the East" (no. 1090): *Ogurosaki Mitsu no Ojima no hito naraba Miyako no tsuto ni iza to iwamashi o,* "If the Islet of Mitsu, at Oguro Cape, were a woman, I'd say, 'Let's go,' to take her as a gift to the City." This poem is a variation on the one cited in note 165.

191   Shitomae no Seki. Shitomae literally means "in front of pissing," with which Bashō plays in the hokku that follows.

192   Ōyama. Not really a mountain but the mountainous part between Shitomae and Sakata.

Samidare o furi-nokoshite ya Hikari-dō
The May rains, falling, seem to spare the Light Hall

L OOKING AT THE NAMBU HIGHWAY IN THE DISTANCE, we stayed in Iwate Village. We passed Oguro Cape[189] and the Islet of Mizu,[190] and as we went from the hot spring of Narugo and reached Shitomae Barrier,[191] we were ready to cross over to the Province of Dewa. Because the road seldom saw travelers, the barrier guard regarded us as suspicious, and it took time before we gained passage. By the time we climbed the Big Mountain,[192] the sun had already set, so we sought lodging in the house of a border guard that we happened to see. For three days the wind and rain were wild, and we had to hole up there in the midst of the dreary mountains.

Nomi shirami uma no barisuru makura moto
Fleas and lice: a horse pisses right near my pillow

Our host said, "From here to Dewa Province beyond the Big Mountain, the road is uncertain. You should have a guide for crossing it." We said, "Surely," and asked for one. A powerfully built young man carrying a curved sword sidewise showed up and, holding an oak cane, he walked ahead

The powerfully built young man.

193 A phrase from Tu Fu's poem, here used only metaphorically.

194 Bashō uses the antiquated term, *shō,* to denote a domain.

195 Suzuki Seifū (1651–1721). A financier and wealthy wholesaler of safflowers, which were used for extracting dyestuff and making cosmetics. He was also a haikai master *(sōshō)* who edited three anthologies. Obanazawa means "Safflower Swamp."

196 In his collection of essays, *Tsurezuregusa,* Yoshida Kenkō (see note 125) observes, "Since ancient times a man of wisdom has rarely been wealthy." In Section 18, where he makes that observation, Kenkō discusses two Chinese men who favored an extremely Spartan approach to life and concludes that such men are highly admired in China, but not in Japan.

197 In reality, for three of the ten days that Bashō and Sora stayed in Obanazawa, beginning on the seventeenth of the fifth month. For the rest, they stayed in Yōsei Temple. The safflower-harvesting season was near, and Seifū was probably very busy.

198 Believing this account, the haikai poet Inazu Gikū (1663–1733), accompanied by another poet, visited Seifū twenty-seven years later, but Seifū declined to be hospitable, saying that he had abandoned haikai for some time and that he could not take in someone without a letter of introduction.

199 The word *nemaru* is a verb in the dialect of the region, which means either "to lie, to sleep" or "to sit." There is a good deal of scholarly investigation into the use of this verb, but one haikai effect is created by its use itself. The kigo is "coolness," which is for summer. In any event, considering that Seifū was probably not adequately hospitable to Bashō and Sora, Bashō may have described in this hokku the comfort he and his friend found in Yōsei Temple. For a sequence beginning with this hokku, see endnote 12.

of us. Worrying, "This has to be the day we definitely run into some danger," we followed him.

Just as our host had said, the high mountains, deeply wooded, did not have a single bird calling that we could hear, and under the overgrowing trees the darkness was such that it was like walking in the night. We felt as if "dust were falling upon us from the tip of the clouds"[193] as we pushed ahead, making sure of each step through the bear bamboo, crossing the streams, stumbling on the rocks, with cold sweat trickling down our bodies, until we came out in the manor[194] of Mogami. The man who had guided us said, "On this road there's always some trouble. I'm glad that I was able to bring you over here without any mishap." We parted in happiness. Even hearing about it after the fact, our hearts throbbed.

IN OBANAZAWA WE VISITED A MAN NAMED SEIFŪ.[195] HE IS wealthy but his heart is not lowly.[196] Someone who goes to the cities from time to time, he of course knew what traveling is like. He made us stay for days,[197] relieving us of the pain of the long trek and entertaining us in various ways.[198]

Suzushisa o waga yado ni shite nemaru kana[199]
Making the coolness our home we lie about

200 This hokku has provoked a great deal of debate on the true meaning of *kaiya*, here given as "silkworm shed," and what the kigo ought to be. In *Man'yō Shū, kaiya* may mean a shed where smoke is generated to repel mosquitoes and deer; it can also be interpreted to mean a structure where something is raised or kept. As for the kigo question, both the toad and silkworm represent spring. To settle the debate, some interpreters say that Bashō was merely describing the height of the silk-making season, which, in the northern part of Japan, falls in summer by the lunar calendar.

201 According to Sora, Bashō composed this hokku after he and Sora left Seifū. Bashō included it in this section as a compliment to his host's business.

202 Sora's diary shows he wrote the initial version of this hokku about the time he and Bashō were visiting Tōkyū, and it read: *Kaiko suru sugata ni nokoru kodai kana,* "The way they raise silkworms recalls ancient days." Bashō revised it and included it in this section as another way of complimenting Seifū.

203 Or Makabe no Heishirō; see note 162.

Hai-ide yo kaiya ga shita no hiki no koe[200]
Crawl out, toad: your voice under the silkworm shed

Mayuhaki o omokage ni shite beni no hana[201]
Recalling the image of the eyebrow brush: the safflower

Kogai suru hito wa kodai no sugata kana[202]   —SORA
Those raising silkworms are in ancient garb

I N THE DOMAIN OF YAMAGATA IS A MOUNTAIN TEMPLE
called Ryūshaku-ji. Founded by the Great Teacher
Jikaku,[203] it is a particularly pure, tranquil place. Because
people urged us to take a look at it, we turned back from
Obanazawa, the distance between them about seven *li*. The
sun was not down yet. After reserving lodging at the visitors'
quarters at the foot we climbed to the temple on the moun-
taintop. The mountain was made of rocks piled upon boul-
ders, the pines and cypresses were aged, and with the soil
and stones old and smooth with moss and the doors of the
lesser halls upon the rocks all closed, we heard not a sound.
As we went around the cliff, crawled up the rocks, and paid
respects to the Buddhist sanctum, the splendid scenery was
so hushed and silent that we could only feel our hearts grow
clear.

204   The initial version: *Yamadera ya iwa ni shimitsuku semi no koe,* "Mountain temple: seeping unto the rocks, the cicada's voice"; a second version: *Sabishisa ya iwa ni shimikomu semi no koe,* "Loneliness: seeping in the rocks, the cicada's voice."

205   Though only about 130 miles long, it is famed as one of the three fastest flowing rivers in Japan.

206   The original for "simple reeds and horns" is *rokaku issei,* probably Bashō's coinage used as a metaphor for lack of culture.

207   Actually, the Mogami originates farther southwest.

208   Goten: an uta-makura. A formation of rocks in the river, so called because they look like the stones used in the game of *go.*

209   Hayabusa: an uta-makura. So called because the rapids are as swift as the falcon.

210   What the *inafune* mentioned in various poems actually meant was subject to debate and conjecture—as in an anonymous tanka "from the East" in *Kokin Shū* (no. 1092): *Mogami-gawa noboreba kudaru inafune no ina niwa arazu kono tsuki bakari,* in which the first seventeen syllables form a *joshi* or *jokotoba,* an introductory phrase, by which *ina* of *inafune* is used to bring out the next *ina,* which means "no." The poem may be paraphrased: "Unlike the *inafune* that's pushed downriver as it tries to go up in the Mogami River because of its rapid flow, I am not saying, '*Ina,*' but am just saying I can't do it this month"—an utterance presumably made by a woman to her boyfriend or suitor. Bashō's observation that *inafune* meant a rice-carrying boat is based on the consensus that had been reached by his time.

211   Shiraito no Taki: an uta-makura. Minamoto no Shigeyuki has a poem: *Mogami-gawa Taki no Shiraito kuru hito no koko ni yoranu wa araji tozo omou,* whose effect (meaning) relies on a pun: *kuru,* which means "to reel in," "to spin (threads)," and "to come." To paraphrase: "Reeling in the White Threads of the Waterfalls of the Mogami River as she comes, the person cannot possibly *not* come by here, I think." The Mogami River is said to have forty-eight such waterfalls.

212   Enshrines Yoshitsune's vassal Hitachino-bō Kaison (dates unknown). *Sennin* means a being with magical powers; the name of the hall derives from the legend that Kaison became such a superhuman being.

Shizukasa ya iwa ni shimiiru semi no koe[204]
Quietness: seeping into the rocks, the cicada's voice

HOPING TO RIDE DOWN THE MOGAMI RIVER,[205] WE waited for good weather at a place called Ōishi-da. Here the seeds of ancient haikai had been spilled, and there were some who kept nurturing the unforgotten flower from the past, trying to soothe their rustic hearts of simple reeds and horns,[206] groping their way with their feet, but they were lost in the two ways of old and new, they said, because they did not have a proper guide. As a result, we ended up doing a sequence. The poetry of this journey culminated in it.

The Mogami River rises in Michinoku, originating as it does in Yamagata.[207] It has terrifyingly dangerous spots such as Go Stones[208] and Falcon.[209] It flows north of Mount Itaji-ki and in the end enters the sea at Sakata. From left and right, mountains close in, and the boat rides down through foliage. The so-called *inafune* must be the boats loaded with rice that ply the waters here.[210] The White-thread Falls[211] splash down through rifts in green leaves. The Sennin Hall[212] stands right at the water's edge. In the brimming water our boat looks precarious.

213   See the Introduction, pp. 27–28, and endnote 13.

214   It is 436 meters (1,300 feet) high and the headquarters of Shugen-dō for its Haguro sect.

215   His haikai name is Rogan (d. 1693). A dyer. *Rogan Kikigaki,* his record of what he heard from Bashō on haikai poetics when he met the master, is deemed valuable.

216   "Acting superintendent" is a tentative translation of *bettō-dai.* Initially, a monk was sent from Edo as superintendent, but by Bashō's time that practice had been abandoned and a local monk was appointed to represent the real one. Ajari (Sanskrit, ācārya) is also a title, given to a ranking monk who acquired enough knowledge to be allowed to teach. Egaku's dates are unknown.

217   Tōyō-in Shion Temple, located midway on the mountain.

218   As is translated, Minamidani means "South Valley," and the hokku recalls "A fragrant wind comes from the south," a phrase from *Zenrin Kushū,* a selection of more than five thousand phrases popular among Zen people originally compiled by Tōyō Eichō (1428–1504). Two earlier versions survive: *Arigata ya yuki o kaorasu kaze no oto,* "Admirable: the sound of a wind making the snow fragrant," and *Arigata ya yuki o megurasu kaze no oto,* "Admirable: the sound of wind making the snow run around." Some commentators argue that the first of these two earlier versions is better than what Bashō selected as final, for the final version is more obvious in praising the holy place. See endnote 14.

219   One account says that Nōjo was the third son of the thirty-second emperor, Sushun, who was assassinated by Soga no Umako, in 592.

220   A Sinified reading of the Province of Dewa. As Bashō goes on to note, the character used for *wa (ha)* of *Dewa* means "feather."

221   This information does not appear in the *Engi-shiki,* a compilation of rules and regulations finished in 927, but in *Azuma Kagami,* for which see the Introduction, p. 19.

222   The surviving *Fudoki*—a collection of topographic reports on various provinces prepared and submitted by government order—does not include a report on Dewa. Bashō may have gotten this information from a temple record.

223   Literally "Mount Moon," it is 1,984 meters (5,950 feet) high. Tsuki-yomi-no-mikoto, the deity of the moon, is enshrined there.

224   Literally "Bath Chamber," it is a peak southwest of Gassan, 1,500 meters (4,500 feet) above sea level. It is famous for its hot springs.

Samidare o atsumete hayashi Mogami-gawa[213]
Gathering the May rains and swift, the Mogami River

ON THE THIRD DAY OF THE SIXTH MONTH WE CLIMBED Mount Haguro.[214] We visited someone named Zushi Sakichi[215] and had the honor of meeting Acting Superintendent Egaku Ajari.[216] He put us up in his detached quarters[217] in Minamidani and served as our host with exquisite pity and compassion.

On the fourth day we held a haikai session in the Main Hall.

Arigata ya yuki o kaorasu Minamidani[218]
Admirable: the snow emitting fragrance in South Valley

On the fifth day we paid our respects to Gongen. It is not known which period the Great Teacher Nōjo, who established this shrine, comes from.[219] The *Engi-shiki* says it is a shrine of Ushū[220] Sato-yama.[221] Did the scribe mistake the character *kuro* for *sato* and call it *sato-yama*? Did he abbreviate Ushū Kuro-yama and call it Haguro-yama? I'm told that the *Fudoki*[222] says that the name Dewa derives from the birds' feathers used as an annual tribute from this province. Along with Gassan[223] and Yudono,[224] it makes up the "three

225   *Shikan*, here given as "insight," is the basic training principle of the Tendai Sect.

226   *Endon yuzū*, here given as "All-round Enlightenment," is the basic goal of the Tendai sect.

227   The original for "rough training and ritual practices" is *shugen gyōbō*. See note 49.

228   A ring made from paper strings hung from the neck.

229   A white cotton cloth wrapped around the head like a turban. Both *yūshime* and *hōkan* are part of the costume for *shugen* practitioners.

230   A legendary spring in China with divine power, which was used by swordsmiths.

mountains." This temple belongs to Tōei-zan Kan'ei Temple, in Edo, and under the bright moon of Tendai Insight[225] it holds up the light of law for All-round Enlightenment.[226] The monks' quarters are lined up roof to roof. The followers of rough training and ritual practices[227] encourage one another in Buddhist ways. The spiritual benefits of this soulful place are such as to fill people with veneration and dread. With its long-lasting prosperity, this holy mountain must be described as felicitous.

On the eighth we climbed Gassan. *Yūshime*[228] hung on our bodies, *hōkan*[229] wrapped around our heads, and led by a mountain guide, we climbed about eight *li* through clouds and mists, treading ice and snow, wondering whether we'd entered the orbits of the sun and the moon. Breathless and frozen, we reached the summit, when the sun set and the moon rose. With bear bamboo spread and short bamboo as pillow, we lay down and waited for the day to break. As the sun rose and clouds dissipated, we went down to Yudono.

Near the valley was a smith's hut. A smith of this province decided to use the spiritual water here, purified himself, and made swords, on which he finally engraved the name Gassan; they are now prized by the whole world. I recalled how swords used to be tempered at Dragon Spring.[230] Thinking

231 A husband-and-wife team of swordsmiths in China. They gave their own names to the pair of swords they collaborated on.

232 Alludes to two lines quoted in *Zenrin Kushū:* "The plantain under the snow is Mo-chieh's painting; / the plum blossoms under the scorching sun are Kian-chai's poetry."

233 Gyōson (1055–1135): *Morotomo ni aware to omoe yamazakura hana yori hoka ni shiru hito mo nashi,* "Let us know each other, mountain cherry: except for your blossoms, I have no one who knows me." This tanka, in *Kin'yō Shū* (Second Version, no. 521) and *Hyakunin Isshu,* comes with a headnote: "Unexpectedly seeing cherries in bloom on Ōmine."

234 The hokku plays with a slight pun, *honomiru,* "to have a faint glimpse of." If the literal meaning of Haguro, "feather black," is also taken into account, the hokku can be paraphrased: "It's nice that it's so cool as we have an occasional glimpse of the crescent over a dark mountain."

235 That is, in gratitude for being able to be in such a spiritual place.

of the days of Kan-chiang and Mo-yeh,[231] I realized how an obsession with the Way could accomplish profound things.

While resting on a rock, I noticed half-open buds on a cherry tree about three feet tall. The way those cherry blossoms, buried under accumulating snow as they had been, were now beginning to bloom though so late, touched me deeply. It was as if plum blossoms were emitting their fragrance right there under the scorching sun.[232] I recalled the sentiments in a poem by Bishop Gyōson,[233] and my feeling intensified. On the whole, the training rules forbid the disclosure of details on this mountain to anyone else. Accordingly, I shall not write any more.

When we returned to the hall, at Ajari's request I wrote out my pieces on our pilgrimage to the three mountains on poem cards.

Suzushisa ya hono mikazuki no Haguro-san[234]
Coolness: a faint three-day moon over Mount Haguro

Kumo no mine ikutsu kuzurete tsuki no yama
Many cloud peaks collapse and the moon over the mount

Katararenu Yudono ni nurasu tamoto kana[235]
In the Bath Chamber I can't speak of I wet my sleeves

The haikai sequence at Tsurugaoka.

236 According to Sora's diary, anyone entering the holy precincts had to surrender all his money and was not allowed to take it back. So the path was littered with coins. The speaker of Sora's hokku is weeping in gratitude for the spirituality of the place—though, as some commentators say, this sentiment strikes the reader as palpably false. According to the same commentators, all of these four hokku are too contrived or forced to be good. It may be argued that a different version of this hokku is better; it reads: *Zeni funde yo o wasurekeri Yudono michi,* "Stepping on coins I forget the world on Yudono path."

237 Some give this name the Sinified reading, Jūkō.

238 See endnote 15.

239 Itō Genjun (1648–97). En'an is his name as a physician and Fugyoku his haikai name.

240 Bashō thanks the host for inviting him to a place with a grand view of the Japan Sea—from Fuku Bay to the north to Mount Atsumi to the south—to enjoy the evening cool. *Yūsuzumi,* here translated as "evening cool," refers to a deliberate act of taking the time out to enjoy the cool breeze in the evening, in the best spot for it. The hokku plays with puns: *atsu* of Atsumi means "hot" and *fuku* of Fuku-ura means "[for wind] to blow." See endnote 16.

241 See endnote 17.

242 When Bashō and Sora visited it, it was a briny lake about two miles long from north to south, over a mile wide east to west, dotted with ninety-nine islets. An earthquake in 1804 raised its bottom, draining most of it. Later visiting the spot, Kobayashi Issa (1763–1827) made a hokku: *Kisakata no kake o tsukande naku chidori,* "Clutching a scrap of the Kisakata marsh plovers cry."

243 This and the following sentences allude to some Chinese verses describing Lake Hsi.

244 Called Dewa Fuji as well as Akita Fuji, it is located about thirteen miles southeast of Kisakata. It consists of an old volcano, 1,635 meters (4,900 feet) high and a new one, 2,236 meters (6,700 feet) high.

Yudono-yama zeni fumu michi no namida kana[236]   —SORA
At Mount Bath Chamber, in tears I step on coins on my way

AFTER LEAVING HAGURO AND ARRIVING IN THE CASTLE town of Tsurugaoka, we were welcomed into the house of a samurai named Shigeyuki,[237] of the Nagayama family, and did a haikai sequence.[238] Sakichi came along with us. We went down to Sakata Port on a riverboat. We stayed in the house of a physician named En'an Fugyoku.[239]

Atsumi-yama ya Fuku-ura kakete yūsuzumi[240]
From Mount Atsumi away to Fuku Bay: evening cool

Atsuki hi o umi ni iretari Mogami-gawa[241]
Pouring the hot sun into the sea, the Mogami River

THOUGH WE HAD SEEN A COUNTLESS NUMBER OF natural wonders on the river, mountain, sea, and land, we were now very eager to see Kisakata.[242] As it lay northeast of Sakata Port, we went over a mountain, walked along the coast, and trod on the sand,[243] for about ten *li*, until, about the time the sun was close to setting, almost hidden in the salty wind swirling up the sand and in the blurring rain, we saw Mount Chōkai.[244] We groped our way

245   The same phrase occurs preceding the two lines quoted from a Su Tung-p'o poem in note 147.

246   In *Go-Shūi Shū* Priest Nōin has a poem he made when he visited Kisakata (no. 519): *Yononaka wa kakutemo hekeri Kisakata no ama no tomaya o waga yado ni shite*, "You can spend this life even in such a manner: a fisherman's hut in Kisakata turned into your home." The island mentioned a little later carries his name because of this poem, not necessarily because he actually lived there.

247   Saigyō has a poem: *Kisakata no sakura wa nami ni uzumorete hana no ue kogu ama no tsuribune*, "Cherries in Kisakata buried by the waves, fishermen row their boats above the blossoms."

248   Mythology has it that as the consort of the fourteenth emperor, Chūai, Jingū conquered Kyushu and Korea. Local legend seems to have said that she passed by this area after her Korean conquest.

249   Muyamuya no Seki: an uta-makura. Its exact location is subject to debate. Also called Uyamuya, Fuyafuya, Moyamoya, Inamuya.

250   Shiokoshi. The shoal that linked Kisakata to the Japan Sea, hence the name. The name also designated Kisakata itself.

in the darkness and, encouraged that because "the rain itself is a spectacle"[245] the clear weather after the rain would be even better, we borrowed space in a fisherman's hut[246] and waited for the rain to let up.

The next morning the sky was very clear. As the morning sun began to shine forth resplendently, we put out in a boat in Kisakata. First, we rowed to Nōin Island and visited the site of his quiet residence of three years. When we climbed out of the boat on the facing shore, the old cherry tree about which a poem was made speaking of "row over the blossoms"[247] remained as a keepsake of Priest Saigyō. Close to the bay was an imperial tomb, which we were told was Empress Jingū's grave. The temple was called Kammanju-ji. I had never heard that she had visited this area. I wondered how the story came about.[248]

When we sat in the temple's main room and rolled up the blind, the entire landscape appeared in a single sweep, with Chōkai pushing up heaven to the south, its shadow reflected in the bay. At the western end was Muyamuya Barrier;[249] to the east was an embankment built with a road leading to Akita in the distance; up to the north was the sea, and the place where the waves rolled in was called the Tide-cross.[250] The bay, its length and width combined, was about one *li*, and though its appearance suggested Matsushima, it also differed from it. Matsushi-

251 *Nebu,* more commonly *nemu,* is the silk tree, which also means "asleep," a pun Bashō plays on, for the original also means "in the rain Hsi-shih is like a flower asleep."

252 Festival at Yuya Gongen, the guardian shrine of Shiokoshi, which Bashō and Sora saw on the seventeenth.

253 In the old days a wooden sliding door was often removed to be used as a seat for several people to enjoy the evening coolness. The description here may also be metaphorical.

254 Probably someone Bashō and Sora happened to meet at the festival mentioned above.

255 Since the Confucian *Odes,* ospreys were the metaphor for uxorious love in the literatures influenced by Chinese classics. This hokku alludes to Kiyohara no Motosuke's tanka cited in note 128.

ma seemed to be smiling, Kisakata resentful. Sadness added to loneliness, the make-up of the place resembled a soul in distress.

Kisakata ya ame ni Seishi ga nebu no hana[251]
In Kisakata in the rain Hsi-shih's silk tree flowers

Shiokoshi ya tsuru hagi nurete umi suzushi
At Tide-cross cranes' shins are wet in the cool sea

Rite[252]

Kisakata ya ryōri nani kuu kami-matsuri   —SORA
In Kisakata what food's eaten at the gods' festival?

Ama no ya ya toita o shikite yū-suzumi[253]
            — Merchant from the Province of Mino   TEIJI[254]
At a fisherman's we sit on a door for evening coolness

Spotting an osprey nest atop a rock

Nami koenu chigiri arite ya misago no su[255]   —SORA
With the vow that waves won't come over the osprey nest

256   May also be translated as the Hokuriku Region; it covers the seven provinces, from the north, of Sado, Echigo, Etchū, Noto, Kaga, Echizen, and Wakasa (today's Niigata, Toyama, Ishikawa, and Fukui).

257   Kanazawa.

258   One of "the three barriers of the East." It was built in 653 as a forward base to fight the Ezo, the northern "barbarians." By Bashō's day it was no more than a police booth.

259   Bashō's error. Ichiburi, then still properly functioning as an official checkpoint, was in Echigo.

260   Actually, it is known that Bashō and Sora took sixteen days to go from Sakata to Ichiburi and fourteen from Nezu Barrier to Ichiburi.

261   The seventh night of the seventh month is Tanabata, a "star festival," which apparently combines a Chinese fable and the Japanese custom of expressing gratitude to the weavers. It is the night when Princess Weaver, represented by the star Vega, is allowed to meet her husband Oxherd, represented by the star Altair. For Oxherd to cross the Milky Way (the River of Heaven) for the meeting, magpies form a bridge with their bodies. On this evening, "strips of paper with poetic effusions in [the couple's] honour being stuck on stems of bamboo grass [are] set up in various places," B. H. Chamberlain observed in *Things Japanese*. As *Awazuhara*, a haikai collection compiled to commemorate the seventeenth anniversary of Bashō's death, put it, "The number of hokku celebrating Tanabata since ancient times can't, in truth, be surpassed by that of the stars." The haikai of Bashō's hokku lies in commending the night before, rather than the night itself. Because of the legend, this hokku suggests "love" in a renga sequence. See also endnote 18.

262   One interesting point made about this hokku is that from Izumozaki, where this is supposed to have been made, the Milky Way does not "lie toward" Sado Island. As many argue, this departure from the actuality should be accepted as an instance of poetic license. See endnote 19.

263   Oya-shirazu, Ko-shirazu, Inu-modori, Koma-gaeshi. Particularly dangerous spots on the passage made on the rocky beach right under cliffs.

A S WE ACCUMULATED DAYS IN OUR INABILITY TO SEP-
arate ourselves from Sakata, we saw the Hokuriku
Route[256] in the clouds. The thought of the great distance
pained our hearts. We heard that it was 130 *li* to the capital
of Kaga.[257] As we passed Nezu Barrier,[258] we stepped into
the land of Echigo and reached Ichiburi Barrier in Etchū.[259]
It took us nine days.[260] My spirit run down by the hardship
of heat and rain, I became ill and could not keep a record.

Fumitsuki ya muika mo tsune no yo niwa nizu[261]
Seventh month: even the sixth isn't like an ordinary night

Araumi ya Sado ni yokotau Amanogawa[262]
Rough sea: lying toward Sado Island the River of Heaven

T ODAY, BECAUSE WE HAD COME OVER THE MOST DIF-
ficult spots in the North Country, called Parent
Ignored, Child Ignored, Dog Going Back, and Horse Turned
Back,[263] we were tired and, pulling our pillows up close to
ourselves, we tried to sleep. From one room beyond, toward
the front, however, I heard the voices of young women, two
of them I thought. As I listened to them telling their stories,
with the voice of an old man interjecting from time to time,
the women turned out to be prostitutes of a place called

The two prostitutes at Ichiburi Barrier.

264 The Grand Shrine of Ise, with Amateraru-Ō-Mi-Kami, the Sun Goddess, presiding, was decreed in 688, by Empress Jitō (645–702), to be completely rebuilt every twenty years. The year of Bashō's journey fell on the year of the rebuilding and many people, without proper permission of parents or employers, visited the shrine. The custom of such visits to Ise, called *nuke-mairi,* was tolerated by all. Of the popularity of this shrine, Luis Frois wrote: "An almost incredible number of people flock from all the kingdoms of Japan in pilgrimage to this *kami* for [she] is the principal one; this multitude includes not only poor and lowly folk but also many noble men and women who have taken a vow to make this pilgrimage. And it even seems that he who does not go there cannot be counted among the ranks of men."

265 Alludes to an anonymous tanka: *Shiranami no yosuru nagisa ni yo o sugusu ama no ko nareba yado mo sadamezu,* "I spend nights on the beach where white waves roll in, a fisherman's child with no place to settle." This tanka appears in the category of "prostitutes" of *Wakan Rōei Shū,* an anthology of verses in Chinese and Japanese compiled by Fujiwara no Kintō (966–1041).

266 Evidently Bashō was dressed like a Buddhist monk.

267 For the Sun Goddess, see note 264.

268 This hokku, along with the passage preceding this, may correspond to a description of "love" in a renga sequence. For some of the points to be considered in interpreting this hokku, see endnote 20.

Niigata, in Echigo Province. They were on their way to pay their respects to Ise Shrine,[264] and the man had accompanied them as far as this barrier. They were trying to write letters to be taken back tomorrow to their home town to convey some ineffectual messages. As if cast up on the beach by white waves, living lowly lives like those of fishermen's children,[265] forced to have faithless relationships, we are, to our great misfortune, committing sinful deeds day after day—such was their talk, and while listening to it, I fell asleep.

The next morning, as we were preparing to leave, they came to us and said in tears: "We're worried about the roads we're taking from now on; we're saddened by so much uncertainty. May we follow you—we'll keep some distance from you. On account of the robe you wear,[266] would you extend Buddha's compassion to us, so we may enter Buddhahood?" However, I had to tell them: "We sympathize with your plight, but we stop in many places. You should go along following the others as they go. With the Sun Goddess's protection,[267] all should go well."

And so we left. Nevertheless, sadness did not cease for quite some time.

Hitotsuya ni yūjo mo netari hagi to tsuki[268]
In one house prostitutes also slept: bush clover and moon

269   No mention of this incident appears in Sora's diary.

270   The Kurobe River divides into many distributaries. Forty-eight is a conventional metaphor for "many."

271   Nago no Ura: an uta-makura. In *Man'yō Shū*, Ōtomo no Yakamochi has a tanka (no. 4018): *Minato kaze samuku fukurashi Nago no E ni tsuma yobi-kawashi tsuru sawa ni naku,* "The harbor wind must be blowing cold: on Nago Bay cranes busily cry, calling out to their wives."

272   An uta-makura. *Man'yō Shū* has a set of four poems in praise of the wisteria flowers on Tako Bay. One of them (no. 4201) is by Kume no Asomi Hirotsuna: *Isasakani omoite koshi o Tako no Ura ni sakeru fuji mite hitoyo henubeshi,* "I hadn't expected much before coming, but having seen the wisteria blooming on Tako Bay, I'd like to stay here for one night."

273   Ariso Umi: an uta-makura. It originally meant "the sea that is rough on the beach"; it then came to designate either the sea around today's Fushiki Harbor, in Toyama, or the larger sea off the coast of the region. *Wase* is a species of rice that ripens early. In *San-zōshi*, Bashō discusses this hokku as an example illustrating the need to describe a sweeping view when writing in praise of an affluent land. At least nominally, Kaga was the greatest producer of rice during the Edo Period, the annual income of its daimyo, the Maeda, put at 1,000,000 *koku* or 5,120,000 bushels.

274   U no Hana Yama: an uta-makura. *Man'yō Shū* has an anonymous tanka (no. 1963): *Kakubakari ame no furaku ni hototogisu U no Hana Yama ni nao ka nakuran,* "When the rain is falling like this, the cuckoo still calls over Mount Deutzia Flower."

275   An ancient battleground. On the eleventh of the fifth month, 1183, Minamoto no Yoshinaka (1154–84), also known as Kiso no Yoshinaka, destroyed the bulk of the Taira clan's central forces by driving them over the cliff into the valley. Bashō felt a special affinity to Yoshinaka, a commander pursued and killed by his own side, and requested to be buried at the temple dedicated to him, Gichū-ji (*Gichū* is a Sinified reading of Yoshinaka).

276   Recorded to have died in 1731. One of his hokku is included in *Sarumino*, an important anthology of the Bashō School published in 1691, and reads: *Sora-tsuri ya kashira furatsuku yuri no hana,* "Bewildering: the way the head of the lily staggers."

277   Today's Osaka.

I told this to Sora, and he wrote it down.[269]

THEY SPEAK OF THE FORTY-EIGHT FLOWS OF KUROBE,[270] and we certainly had to cross countless rivers before coming out on a bay called Nago.[271] It doesn't have to be spring to appreciate the wisteria flowers of Tako;[272] one can also visit their sad decline in early fall, we thought, and asked someone about them and were told, "You'll have to walk along the beach about five *li* from here until you reach the foothill woods beyond. Still, there are only shabby fishermen's thatched huts there, and no one will be willing to give you lodging even for one night." Intimidated, we went on to enter the province of Kaga.

Wase no ka ya wake-iru migi wa Ariso Umi[273]
We wade into early rice fragrance, the Rough Sea to our
   right

GOING OVER MOUNT DEUTZIA FLOWER[274] AND KURI-kara Valley,[275] we reached Kanazawa on the midpoint day of the seventh month. Here, there was a merchant named Kasho,[276] a frequent visitor from Ōzaka.[277] We stayed in the same inn.

278 Kosugi Isshō (1653–88). A tea dealer, he was widely anthologized. The haikai name Isshō means "one laugh."

279 Haikai no renga.

280 Haikai name Besshō.

281 The pieces by the participants in this session, held on the twenty-second of the seventh month, were collected and published, in 1691, under the title of *Nishi no Kumo*. Sora notes he had to leave early because of illness.

282 By a gentleman named Saitō Issen, on the twentieth of the seventh month.

283 *Nishi no Kumo* lists an earlier version: *Zansho shibashi tegoto ni ryōre uri nasubi*, "Heat persists awhile: cook melons, eggplants, each to his own liking." *Zansho*, "remaining heat," is a kigo for the early part of autumn, which, by the lunar calendar, begins in the seventh month.

284 Thought to be on the way to Kanazawa. The hokku that follows may have been made around the thirteenth of the seventh month.

285 A lament over the sun that continues to be hot despite the arrival of autumn by the calendar.

286 Komatsu.

287 This hokku is judged to be syntactically ambiguous because of the awkward use of the verb *fuku*, "to blow." A sequence of forty-four links, called *yoyoshi*, was completed with this as hokku, with ten participants. According to Sora, this session was held on the twenty-fifth, after the visit to Ōta Shrine described in the following passage. See endnote 21.

Someone named Isshō[278] had begun to be fairly well known among those of like mind as one fond of this pursuit,[279] but had died young, in the previous winter. His brother[280] hosted a session in commemoration:[281]

Tsuka mo ugoke waga naku koe wa aki no kaze
Gravestone, move: sound of my wailing the autumn wind

Invited to a Certain Grass Hut[282]

Aki suzushi tegoto ni muke ya uri nasubi[283]
Autumn's cool: let each of us peel a melon, an eggplant

On the Way[284]

Akaaka to hi wa tsurenaku mo aki no kaze[285]
Red and red: the sun's indifferent to the autumn wind

At a Place Called Little Pine[286]

Shiorashiki na ya komatsu fuku hagi susuki[287]
Daintily named Little Pine blowing bush clover, pampas grass

288 Minamoto no Sanemori (1111–83). His initial allegiance was to the leader of the clan, Yoshitomo (1123–60), but he switched it to one of the leaders of the rival Taira clan, Munemori (1147–85). For a battle with Minamoto no Yoshinaka (note 275), he dyed his white hair black to conceal his age; he was killed. Yoshinaka, who had glimpsed him when young, pitied him for this turn of events and held a memorial service for him. Zeami (1364?–1443) wrote a nō play called *Sanemori*.

289 Sanemori wore a tunic of red brocade under his armor for his last battle. This he did with Munemori's special permission.

290 A metal decoration on the front side of the crown.

291 For victory.

292 One of Yoshinaka's *shiten'nō*, "four guardian kings." As the Sanemori section of *The Tale of the Heike* (Book VII) tells it, Jirō, who knew Sanemori well, identified a head brought back from battle as Sanemori's. In the hokku that follows, Bashō uses Jirō's exclamation when he sees Sanemori's head: *Ana muzan ya*, "Oh, how cruel!"

293 *Engi*, a historical account of a shrine or temple.

294 With an earlier version of this hokku, a sequence of thirty-six links was completed. See endnote 22.

295 Shirane ga Dake: an uta-makura. Also known as Shiro-yama, "White Mountain."

296 The sixty-fourth emperor (968–1008). After being forced to retire through his courtiers' scheming, he went on pilgrimage to various places.

297 The thirty-three spiritual places in the western region. The pilgrimage begins with Nachi, in Kii, and ends with Tanigumi, in Mino.

298 Daiji Daihi or Kanzeon Bosatsu (Avalokiteśvara). The Sanskrit name means "the Lord who looks down upon the world with compassion" or "he who is looked up to for help."

HERE WE PAID OUR RESPECTS TO ŌTA SHRINE. IT HAD Sanemori's[288] helmet, along with a strip of brocade.[289] Long ago, while he still belonged to the Minamoto clan, Lord Yoshitomo gave it to him, we were told. It certainly wasn't one for an ordinary soldier. From visor to side-guard, it had gold-speckled arabesque engravings in the chrysanthemum pattern, and the dragon head[290] had antlers riveted to it. After Sanemori was killed in battle, Kiso Yoshinaka donated it to this shrine with a letter of prayers,[291] with Higuchi no Jirō[292] as messenger— so said the official account[293] vividly.

Muzan ya na kabuto no shita no kirigirisu[294]
Cruel: under the helmet a cricket

ON OUR WAY TO THE HOT SPRINGS OF YAMANAKA, WE walked with Shirane Peak[295] at our back. In the foothills to the left was Kannon Hall. After Cloistered Emperor Kazan[296] completed his pilgrimage to the Thirty-three Places,[297] he built a house for a statue of Great-compassion-great-sorrow[298] and named it Nata, they said. We were told that the name was made from the two characters that begin with Nachi and Tanigumi. With oddly shaped stones arranged variously and surrounded by old pines, it

The departure of Sora.

299 It is often noted that here the *ishiyama*, "stone mountain," is the mountain with the same name in Ōmi where Ishiyama Temple is located. However, the interpretation that Bashō was merely describing what he saw may be more persuasive. In traditional Chinese perception, the color for autumn is white.

300 In Hyōgo, also famous for its hot springs.

301 Alludes to a Chinese legend about a boy named Tz'u-t'ung who lived in exile for seven hundred years by drinking the dew on chrysanthemums. The suggestion is that one could live as long by taking this hot bath. See endnote 23.

302 The boyhood name of Izumiya Jinzaemon (1676–1751).

303 Yasuhara Masaaki (1610–73), one of "the seven haikai saints" of the Teimon School.

304 Matsunaga Teitoku (1571–1653), the founder of the Teimon School of haikai.

was a small hall with a thatched roof built against a rock—
this, a wonderful, gratifying land.

Ishiyama no ishi yori shiroshi aki no kaze[299]
Whiter than the stones of the stone mountain the autumn
wind

WE BATHED IN A HOT SPRING. WE HEARD THAT ITS
efficacy was second only to that of Arima.[300]

Yamanaka ya kiku wa taoranu yu no nioi[301]
In Yamanaka I don't break mums off in hot water's scent

The proprietor, named Kumenosuke,[302] was still a boy.
His father was fond of haikai. When Teishitsu,[303] of Kyoto,
was a young man, he came here and was so embarrassed by
his ignorance of poetry that upon his return to Kyoto he
became a disciple of Teitoku[304] and he began to be known.
Even after his reputation was established, he would not
accept judge's fees in this village. This is now an old story.

SORA DEVELOPED STOMACH TROUBLE AND, BECAUSE
he had a relative in a place called Nagashima, in the
province of Ise, went ahead, leaving me with:

305 The kigo is *hagi*, "bush clover," which is for autumn. See *A Farewell Gift to Sora*.

306 Alludes to Su Wu's farewell poem for Li Ling: "Two wild ducks flew north together; / one alone now soars southward." Burton Watson, trans., *Meng Ch'iu: Famous Episodes from Chinese History and Legend* (Kodansha International, 1979), p. 28.

307 The kigo is *tsuyu*, "dew," which is for autumn. The *kakitsuke*, "inscript" or "inscription," refers to one of the standard writings on the traveler's hat, such as "The two of us have no fixed residence in all the universe." One of the two is Buddha. In *Oi no Kobumi* Bashō says he used this inscription in 1688 when he traveled briefly with his favorite friend Tsuboi Tokoku (d. 1690). A rich rice dealer, Tokoku was suspected of business irregularities and exiled.

308 Li Ling's farewell poem ends with: "Drifting clouds, each day a thousand miles— / how can you know the sorrow in my heart?" *Meng Ch'ieu*, p. 27.

Yukiyukite taore fusu tomo hagi no hara[305]   —SORA

In the end I might collapse, but in a field of bush clover

The one going saddened, the one left behind despondent, we were like single ducks after parting, lost in clouds.[306] I added:

Kyō yori wa kakitsuke kesan kasa no tsuyu[307]

From today on, erase the inscript, dew on my hat

I STAYED IN A TEMPLE CALLED ZENSHŌ-JI OUTSIDE THE castle town of Daishōji. It was still in the domain of Kaga. Sora, who had also stayed in this temple the previous night, had left this piece:

Yomosugara akikaze kiku ya ura no yama

All night long I hear the autumn wind on the mountain
   in back

The separation of a single night was equal to that of a thousand *li*.[308] Listening to the autumn winds, I lay in the quarters for training monks. Near daybreak, as the voices of sutra chanting rose in the sky, the gong rang out, and I entered the dining hall. Eager with the thought that I would

At the temple Zenshō-ji.

309 Shiokashi no Matsu: the pine trees surrounding Shiokoshi Shrine.

310 Though often attributed to Saigyō, this tanka was actually composed by Ren'nyo (1415–99).

311 A phrase in *Chuang Tzu*.

enter the province of Echizen today, I hurried out of the temple. Young monks followed me, carrying inkstones and paper down to the staircase. As it happened, the willow in the garden was scattering its leaves:

Niwa haite ideba ya tera ni chiru yanagi
> As I sweep the garden and walk out, willow leaves
> scatter

I dashed this off impromptu with my straw sandals on.

ON THE BORDER OF ECHIZEN, I PUT OUT IN A BOAT IN the inlet of Yoshizaki and poled myself to visit the Tide-cross Pines.[309]

Yomosugara arashi ni nami o hakobasete
tsuki o taretaru Shiokoshi no matsu —SAIGYŌ[310]
> All night long with the storm carrying the waves,
> the Tide-cross Pines drip the moon

In this one poem are all the views described. One word added would be like "a useless finger implanted."[311]

312 Monk Daimu (dates unknown), who used to be the resident monk of Tenryū Temple, in Shinagawa, Edo.

313 Tachibana Hokushi (d. 1718). A participant in *A Farewell Gift to Sora*. Counted among "the ten top disciples" of Bashō, he recorded Bashō's observations on haikai during this visit in *Yamanaka Mondō* (Questions and Answers in Yamanaka). The booklet was not published until 1862, however.

314 Since the arrival of cool autumn obviates the need for fans, *ōgi oku*, "to set aside a fan," and *sute ōgi*, "an abandoned fan," are the standard kigo for early autumn. An early version of this hokku read: *Mono kakite ōgi hegi-wakuru wakare kana*, "I write on a fan and tear the sheet off as we part"—meaning tearing one of the two sheets that make up a fan. Hokushi followed it with *warōte kiri ni kioi ideba ya*, "laughing I set out into the mist newly resolved." In both of Bashō's versions, "tearing" is a metaphor for giving a hokku as a farewell gift.

315 The founder of Sōtō Zen in Japan (1200–53).

316 An established haikai poet in Fukui. His dates are not known.

IVISITED THE RESIDENT MONK[312] OF TENRYŪ TEMPLE, IN Maruoka, whom I had known previously. Also, someone named Hokushi,[313] of Kanazawa, intending to accompany me briefly, ended up coming as far as this, unable to separate. He tried to compose a hokku at all the notable sites, without overlooking a single one, and from time to time recited an interesting one to me. When the time to part finally came:

Mono kakite ōgi hikisaku nagori kana[314]
I write on a fan and tear it apart, lingering

I walked into the mountain about five thousand yards to offer prayers at Eihei Temple. It is Zen Master Dōgen's.[315] He avoided the vicinity of Kyoto, I was told, and chose to leave his traces at foothills like this for some unfathomable reason.

IT WAS ONLY THREE *LI* TO FUKUI, SO I SET OUT AFTER finishing supper, but I found the road at dusk rough going.

In this place lived an ancient hermit named Tōsai.[316] Which year was it, he had come to Edo to visit me. It was about ten years ago. Wondering how much more ancient he

The house of the ancient hermit Tōsai.

317 *Yūgao.* This passage is a haikai compression of the *Yūgao* chapter of *The Tale of Genji.* See endnote 24.

318 *Hahakigi,* literally "broom tree," which is also the title of one of the chapters of *The Tale of Genji.* In *Genji,* it refers to a legendary tree that you are supposed to be able to see when you are far away but not when you are close to it. Here, it more likely refers to a weedy plant with the same name, also known as *hōki-gusa.*

319 Alludes to a sentence in *Yūgao:* "'I've heard something like this only in an old story,' Genji thought, mystified."

320 Asamuzu no Hashi: an uta-makura. There is an ancient *Saibara* song called *Asamuzu,* which can mean "morning water" or "shallow water," depending on the Chinese characters applied. Taking the latter meaning, the song may be translated: "The Shallow-water Bridge rumbles, rumbles. / The rain has fallen, and I've fallen away. / Who on earth would pick a go-between / to carry a letter to tell me what the person's like to ask what I think? / Come, noble ones!"

321 Tamae no Ashi: an uta-makura. In *Go-Shūi Shū* Minamoto no Shigeyuki has a tanka on summer (no. 219): *Natsu-kari no Tamae no ashi o fumishidaki mureiru tori no tatsu sora zo naki,* "Trampling on the summer-harvested Tamae reeds, crowding, the birds have no sky to fly up into." The meaning of this poem is subject to debate.

322 Uguisu no Seki: an uta-makura.

323 Yuno'o Tōge. A battlefield where Yoshinaka fought.

324 One of Yoshinaka's forts.

325 Kaeru-yama: an uta-makura. An anonymous poem on traveling in *Gosen Shū* (no. 1335) that has a headnote, "Someone I knew very well abruptly went off to Koshi Province, so I made this poem as a farewell gift": *Ware o nomi omoi Tsuruga no Ura naraba Kaeru no yama wa madowazaramashi,* which uses puns. To paraphrase, "If you think only of me and are only going as far as Tsuruga Bay, you won't be lost when you come back over Mount Return."

must have become or if he might even be dead by now, I made an inquiry and was told that he still lived on in such and such a place.

Away from the busy part of town, his was a small, miserable house overgrown with moonflowers[317] and snake gourds, its doorway hidden behind cockscombs and broom goosefoots.[318] Deciding this must be it, I knocked on the gate, and a lonesome-looking woman came out and said, "I don't know where you are from, sir, but you look like an itinerant priest. The owner went to visit so-and-so in this neighborhood. If you have some business with him, please go see him there." So I guessed she must be his wife. Marveling how an atmosphere like this is possible only in an old story,[319] I soon found him and stayed in that house for two nights, after which I hurried out hoping to see the full moon in Tsuruga Port. To see me off, Tōsai merrily set out with me, the skirts of his kimono tucked up in a funny way, saying he'd be my guide on the road.

IN TIME SHIRANE PEAK HID ITSELF AND HINA PEAK emerged. When I crossed Asamuzu Bridge,[320] the Reeds of Tamae[321] had tufts out. Past Bush Warbler Barrier[322] and down Yuno'o Pass,[323] I heard the season's first wild geese over Hiuchi Castle[324] and Mount Return[325] and, on

326 "Less certain," etc., is a line from a poem by Sun Ming-fu.

327 The preeminent shrine in Echizen.

328 The fourteenth emperor; largely mythological.

329 Ta'a (1237–1319). Yugyō, literally "pilgrimage," refers, as a proper noun, either to the founder of the Ji sect of Buddhism, Ippen (1239–89), as it does here, or to Ta'a, who founded the Yugyō school within the Ji sect.

330 Just before Bashō's visit, Son'nin, Yugyō XXXXIV, had performed the annual ritual.

the evening of the fourteenth, sought an inn in the port town of Tsuruga.

THAT NIGHT THE MOON WAS PARTICULARLY FINE. "Will the moon be like this tomorrow, too?" I asked, and the proprietor said, as he offered sake, "Across this Koshi region, we are even less certain whether it's going to be fine or cloudy tomorrow night."[326]

So I paid a night visit to Kehi Shrine.[327] It is the mausoleum of Emperor Chūai.[328] The shrine looked divinely ancient, and with the moon shining in through the pine trees, the white sand before the deity was like frost spread out.

"Long ago, the holy man Yugyō II[329] made a great resolution and himself cut the grass, carried mud and stones, and drained the muddy swamp. So now there's no more trouble for those who come to pay their respects. That ancient example still lives today, and each holy man carries sand to the sacred place before the deity. It is called 'Yugyō's sand-carrying,'" explained my host.

Tsuki kiyoshi Yugyō no moteru suna no ue[330]
The moon is clear above the sand Yugyō has carried

On the fifteenth day it rained as my host had predicted.

331 Small clams with pink or yellowish brown shells.

332 Iro no Hama. The name may derive from Saigyō's tanka: *Shio somuru masuho no kogai hiroutote Iro no Hama to wa iu ni ya aruramu,* "Because they pick small *masuho* shells that dye the tides, they must call the place Colored Beach."

333 Actually, about three *li*.

334 Ten'ya Gorōemon (dates unknown), a shipper. Sora says that, arriving there first, he entrusted Ten'ya with a letter to Bashō and notified him of the poet's imminent arrival; in response, Ten'ya provided the entertainment. Sora himself did not meet Ten'ya.

335 Suma is famous for autumnal desolation.

336 The account remains at the temple. See endnote 25.

Meigetsu ya Hokukoku biyori sadamenaki
Full moon: the weather in the North Country is unreliable

O N THE SIXTEENTH DAY, WITH THE SKY CLEAR,
desiring to pick some small *masuho* shells,[331] we
hurried a boat to Colored Beach.[332] It was seven *li* over the
water.[333] Ten'ya so-and-so[334] had lunch baskets and bamboo
sake tubes prepared with care and attention and, a number
of his servants riding in the boat and a tailwind driving us,
we were blown to the shore in no time. It had only a few
small houses of fishermen and the forlorn-looking Hokke
Temple. There we drank tea and warmed sake to endure the
loneliness of the evening.

Sabishisa ya Suma ni kachitaru hama no aki [335]
The loneliness here's superior to Suma, autumn on the
beach

Nami no ma ya kogai ni majiru hagi no chiri
In the waves, mixing with small shells bush clover litter

I had Tōsai write down a brief account of the day and left it
at the temple.[336]

Meeting with Sora and Rotsū at Ōgaki.

337 Iwabe Yojiemon (1649–1738). A wandering beggar poet who was initially scheduled to accompany Bashō on this journey. His haikai name Rotsū means either "dewy passage" or "road passage," depending on the Chinese characters applied.

338 Ochi Jūzō (b. 1656), a merchant.

339 Kondō was his family name. He renounced his samurai status early and became a monk. A haikai judge, he died around 1706.

340 His family name was Tsuda (dates unknown). A samurai of the Ōgaki fiefdom.

341 Miyazaki Tazaemon (d. 1725). He served the Ōgaki fiefdom for fifty-two years before retiring. All three of his sons became members of Bashō's school.

342 In at least two of three *dempon*, "transmitted editions," this hokku is lineated in this manner. See endnote 26.

R OTSŪ³³⁷ HAD COME AS FAR AS THIS PORT TO WELCOME me back and accompanied me to the province of Mino. As I entered the manor of Ōgaki, assisted by a horse, Sora came from Ise to join us. Etsujin³³⁸ galloped his horse to do the same, and we all gathered in Jokō's³³⁹ house. Zensenshi,³⁴⁰ Keikō³⁴¹ and his sons, and others who are close to me came to visit day and night and, as if meeting someone who had returned to life, expressed joy and consolation. Even before I was able to shake off the weariness of my travels, the sixth day of the ninth month came along, so I decided to offer prayers at the rebuilding of Ise Shrine and put myself on a boat again:

Hamaguri no
   futami ni
      *wakare yuku aki zo*³⁴²

A clam
   separates lid
      from flesh as autumn departs

ENDNOTES

1   Early in 1689, Bashō wrote Kubota Ensui (1660–1704), a well-to-do merchant in his home town, Iga. Part of the letter reads:

> ... Last fall I accompanied a demented man named Etsujin on the Kiso route, risking my life on suspension bridges, unable to console myself at Obasute, hearing fulling mallets and clappers, watching people driving deer off, and, as I dwelt on these things that affected me so, I only thought of you. Even as the new year has come around, I cannot stop the thoughts of traveling:
>
> *Ganjitsu wa ta-goto no hi koso koishikere*   —BASHŌ
> On New Year's Day, in each rice paddy I miss the sun
>
> When the third month comes, I plan to visit the North Country beginning around the time of the cherry in Shiogama, the blurred moon over Matsushima, and the *katsumi* blooming in Asaka Swamp, all of which I've been eager to see, so that I may turn up in Mino and Owari by the start of autumn or at the latest by winter. If my dewy life manages to last long enough, I'd like to see you again, if only by stopping by and standing around; I think of this prospect with joy. I feel as if our parting in the southern city [i.e., Nara] had taken place a whole generation ago, but I find it hard to forget the transience of a single night, the tears at a single hut [that we shared], and cannot leave aside the idea [of traveling], obsessed as I am

that life fades like foam on the water. Since last year's
travels I've been brushing aside fish and meat from
my mouth, thinking with fondness of the places that
noble monk traced, who exclaimed with desolation
that living a mendicant's life, with a single begging
bowl, would be more admirable, and I am determined,
in traveling this year, to be sparing, sparing about
myself, ready to wear a straw-coat. . . .

"Demented man," *shiremono,* is a deprecatory endear-
ment. Bashō had met Ensui last, in Nara, on the eighth of
the fourth month of the previous year. For *katsumi,* see p. 63.
The "noble monk" refers to Zōga (917-1003), a priest of the
Tendai sect who avoided worldly advancements and any
involvement with the court by pretending to be insane. Leg-
end has it that when a fellow priest was promoted to bishop
and made his pleasure known, Zōga showed up in tattered
clothes and exclaimed, "Such worldly fame is painful, being
a beggar is more pleasurable!"

2   Contrast this description of the departure with that in *Oi no
Kobumi.*

In early Godless Month the sky looked uncertain and
I, like a leaf in the wind, felt as if I did not know
where I was going:

Tabibito to waga na yobaren hatsu-shigure
I'd like to be called a traveler in the first shower

mata sazanka o yado-yado ni shite
again lodging under sasanqua from place to place

A resident of Iwaki by the name of Chōtarō came
up with this waki as people threw a send-off party for
me at Kikaku's house.

Toki wa fuyu Yoshino o komen tabi no tsuto
Time's winter: may Yoshino be the travels' message

This hokku was given me by Lord Rosen as the
first of the farewell gifts; my old friends, close and not
so close, and my disciples came to visit with Chinese
poems, tanka, and other writings, some showing
goodwill by presenting me with monies for sandals
wrapped in paper. I did not have to make any efforts
to "collect three-month's worth of food." Because they
gave me a paper-garment and cotton clothes, a cap
and socks, from each a different item, I did not have
to worry about pain from the cold of frost and snow.
Some put out a boat, some entertained me at their
villas, and some brought sake and tidbits to my grass
hut to toast for my trip; all these people found our
parting hard, as if I were someone of distinction going
away, and I was truly overwhelmed.

"Godless Month," *Kannazuki,* is another name for the
tenth month, by the lunar calendar the first winter month.
The "first shower," *hatsu-shigure,* refers to the sudden, brief
shower that presages the onset of winter; "uncertain,"
sadame naki, is a conventional description of the meteoro-
logical phenomenon. Rosen (Dew Wet) is a haikai name of
Naitō Yoshihide (1655–1733), the second son of the
daimyo Naitō Yoshiyasu (1619–85), whose haikai name is
Fūko (Wind Tiger); both son and father helped poetry
flourish in their fiefdom. Rosen's hokku is an example of
extreme compression and expresses the hope that Bashō
will bring back a hokku or two on Yoshino, which he is
scheduled to visit in the spring. Yoshino is famous for cher-
ry blossoms. To "collect three-month's worth of food" is a
phrase in *Chuang Tzu.*

Yamamoto Satoshi, who traced the route Bashō and Sora
took step by step, notes the discrepancies between the open-
ing passage of the *Oku no Hosomichi* and Sora's diary and

speculates that Bashō spent far more time than is suggested there on a variety of farewell parties held for him.

3   Yashima, "Eight Islands," is said to have been the name of a kitchen deity at one time, although I have not seen any explanation that links this meaning to the set of eight three-legged cauldrons built in the Palace Kitchen, which was called Yashima no Kanae, *kanae* being a tripod cauldron. Muro no Yashima was at one time the name of the rite performed on the night of the last day of the year in front of a cleaned oven to divine the fortune of the coming year. In this phrase, *muro* probably means "monastery" or "chamber."

Meanwhile, Muro no Yashima came to be accepted as an uta-makura in the province of Mutsu because Fujiwara no Sanekata (d. 998) referred to it in a tanka on love, which is included in *Shika Shū* (no. 188):

> *Ikade kawa omoi ari tomo shirasubeki Muro no Yashima no*
> *kemuri naradewa*
> I think of you but how could I let you know, I not
>   being the smoke from Muro no Yashima?

Also, Sanekata died while governor of Mutsu, thereby spawning legendary tales. However, in another poem Sanekata speaks of a Muro no Yashima having been stolen, in which case he may have been referring to one of the kitchen cauldrons mentioned above. The Yashima no Kanae plays a role in the passage about Counselor Isonokami in *Taketori Monogatari* (Tale of the Bamboo Cutter), Japan's oldest extant full-length fiction that is thought to have taken its present form in the late ninth century.

When Muro no Yashima, as an uta-makura, was linked to Ōmiya Shrine, it was explained that Yashima referred to the eight islets on the pond in the shrine precinct and "the smoke" in Sanekata's poem to the vapor rising from the pond.

4   Sora, who studied Shintoism with Kitsukawa Koretaru (1616–94), had enough knowledge about Shinto-related places to provide the kind of explanation he gave to Bashō during their visit to Muro no Yashima.

The account in the *Kojiki* passage describing Ama-tsu-hiko-hiko-ho-no-ninigi-no-mikoto, the Sun Goddess's grandson, differs substantially from that in the *Nihon Shoki*. Ama-tsu-hiko-hiko-ho-no-ninigi-no-mikoto is given the task of descending from the heavens to rule the Central Land of the Reed Plains. Because of this, he is called the *sume-mima*, "offspring of the heavenly deities" (in Donald Philippi's definitive translation of *Kojiki*, Princeton University Press and University of Tokyo Press, 1968). In my translation of the shorter *Nihon Shoki* version, he will be identified as "the heavenly grandson."

When Ama-tsu-hiko-hiko-ho-no-ninigi-no-mikoto arrived at Cape Kasasa, in Nagano, Ata:

There was a man there. He called himself Kotokatsu Kunikatsu Nagasa. The heavenly grandson asked, "Is there a country or not?" What the man said in response was, "There is a country here, sire. I hope you will do whatever you please with it." Accordingly, he went and stayed there.

There happened to be a beautiful woman in that country. Her name was Kashi-tsu-hime. Another name was Kamu-ata-tsu-hime. Another name was Ko-no-hana-saku-ya-bime. The heavenly grandson asked this beautiful woman, "Whose child are you?" What she said in response was, "I am the child born when a heavenly deity married Ō-yama-tsu-no-kami and begat." Accordingly, the heavenly grandson summoned her. She became pregnant in one night. Feeling deceived, the heavenly grandson said, "A heavenly deity I may be, but how can I make a human being pregnant in one night? What you have in your belly can't possibly be my child."

Furious and resentful, Kashi-tsu-hime made a doorless chamber and shut herself in it, swearing, "If what I have in my belly is not the heavenly grandson's child, he's bound to burn up and be destroyed. If he is truly the heavenly grandson's child, even fire won't be able to damage him." Thereupon she set fire to the chamber.

She named the child she bore at the end of the smoke that arose first Ho-no-suseri-no-mikoto. He is the ancestor of the hayato. She named the child she bore next while she was sitting avoiding the heat Hiko-ho-ho-de-mi-no-mikoto. She named the child she bore next Ho-no-akari-no-mikoto. He is the ancestor of the Owari tribe. There were three children in all.

In the *Oku no Hosomichi* translation, Ko-no-hana-saku-ya-bime, one of two alternative names of Kashi-tsu-hime, is given as Princess-to-make-trees-bloom. (For the close phonetic interpretation of each name, see the glossary of Philippi's *Kojiki*. If you do so, first read the story in question, on pp. 144–47. Because Philippi follows a more precise system of phonetic transliteration than I do, you will have difficulty finding what corresponds to my transliterations in his glossary.)

5 Opinions differ as to why the fish was banned in the region. One local history reports the custom of broiling it and offering it to the deity, suggesting that it was a sacred fish, whereas one theory seeks the cause of the ban in the notion that this fish, when broiled, smelled like a human corpse during cremation and that any association of *konoshiro* with the legend of the princess was sacrilegious.

Another theory sees the cause of the ban in the legend linking the olfactory notoriety of the fish with the homonymic meaning of *konoshiro*, "child substitute." According to the legend, a powerful man saw a beautiful young woman and threatened to make her his, even though she was in love with another man. When her father learned of this, he burnt a quantity of these fish to pretend that he was cremating his daughter, who he let on had committed suicide in despair. He succeeded in deceiving the obnoxious man while letting his daughter elope with her true love. Following this legend, of which there are said to be many variations, the connection between the fish and the "smoke" could be made, but the banning of the fish does not necessarily follow.

6   The haibun entitled *Snowball* reads as follows:

> Sora so-and-so set up temporary residence near me, and we visit each other mornings and evenings. When I prepare food, he helps add kindling, and the nights when I boil tea, he comes to knock on the door. By nature he prefers seclusion and doesn't allow money to get in the way of friendship. One night, he visited me in the snow:
>
> *Kimi hi o take yoki mono misen yukimaroge*
> You, make a fire; I'll show you something nice: a
>   snowball

7   Seizing on the by then standard Zen interpretation of Bashō's most famous hokku, *Furuike ya kawazu tobikomu mizu no oto*, "An old pond: a frog jumps into the water the sound," in 1868 Kitsuda Shunko (1815–86) concocted a hoax and published it under the title, *Bashō-ō Furuike Shinden* (A True History of the Venerable Bashō's Old Pond). It features a typical Zen dialogue that is supposed to have taken place between Butchō and Bashō, here identified by his early haikai pen name, Tōsei (Peach Green/Blue):

> The elder monk Butchō, of Kompon Temple in Kashima, Jōshū, was a widely read and enlightened man of wisdom. He was an old teacher of the venera-

ble Tōsei. When he transferred to Chōkei Temple in Fukagawa, Edo, he decided to visit Tōsei, accompanied by Rokuso Gohei. When they reached the Bashō hut, Rokuso Gohei first stepped into the hut and asked, "What is the Buddhist Law in the grasses and trees of this quiet garden?" Tōsei replied by saying, ・ "Large leaves are large, small leaves are small." Then the Elder entered the gate and asked, "How is it lately?" Tōsei replied by saying, "A shower has passed and washed the green moss." The Elder asked again, "What was the Buddhist Law before the green moss was born and before the spring rain was yet to come?" At that instant a frog at the rim of the pond leapt and plunged to the bottom of the water. In response to that sound, Tōsei replied, "A frog jumps in—the sound of water." The elder monk Butchō chanted, "Well done! Well done!" and endowed Tōsei with the back scratcher he was carrying.

Why a back scratcher? Because this instrument, called *nyoi*, "at will," was—and perhaps still is—part of an itchy Zen monk's paraphernalia.

8   One of the three sets began with "The start of poetry: a rice-planting song in the Interior." The first three links of this sequence may be translated as follows:

Fūryū no hajime ya Oku no taue-uta   —BASHŌ
The start of poetry: a rice-planting song in the Interior

ichigo o otte waga mōke gusa   —TŌKYŪ
strawberries gathered and set on grass

mizu sekite hirune no ishi ya naosuran   —SORA
damming water he adjusts the stone for a daytime nap

Bashō and Tōkyū make a typical exchange between guest of honor and host—with Bashō thanking Tōkyū for inviting him to such a poetic place and Tōkyū apologizing for his inability to do any more than pick wild strawberries and offer them on weeds to entertain the honored guest. Then Sora shifts the scene by reinterpreting Tōkyū's description, changing it from self-deprecation to the self-satisfaction of a man of leisure. This renga of thirty-six links was completed and survives.

As for the two other sequences, one started by Sora, the other by Tōkyū, only the first three links remain. It is not known whether the first three links were all there are or if they are fragments of a completed sequence.

9   Bashō composed two haibun, both called *Moji-zuri-ishi* (Letter-Rubbing Stone), for this hokku. One of them reads:

In Shinobu Village, in Shinobu County, there is a stone about twelve by twelve feet that is associated with the legend of "letter-rubbing." I hear that long ago a woman's thoughts turned into this stone and that it has letters on its surface. Because dyeing with wild indigo creates chaotic figures, many have made poems comparing them to love. Now the stone is buried in a valley, with its upper surface turned to the ground, so one can't see anything particularly poetic about it. Still, I couldn't think of the past without some nostalgia:

Sanae toru temoto ya mukashi Shinobu-zuri
The hands taking seedlings recall the ancient rubbing

Among the more famous poems on the subject is a tanka on love by Minamoto no Tōru (822–95):

Michinoku no Shinobu moji-zuri tare yue ni midare somenishi ware naranakuni

which may be translated, very limply,

In Michinoku those Shinobu-rubbed figures yes: for
whom else could I have grown as wild?

or, taking *shinobu* to mean the dye plant,

The dye with hare's-foot fern, of Michinoku—who
else would have made me feel so disturbed?

The poem is included in *Kokin Shū* (no. 724).

10   The authenticity of this Tsubo no Ishibumi is questioned.
In the first place, there was a different marker also called
by that name. As described in *Shūchū Shō*, a treatise on poet-
ics by Fujiwara no Kenshō (b. ca. 1130), it was the one on
which General Sakanoue no Tamuramaro (758–811), the
first subjugator of the Ezo, is reputed to have chiseled the
characters *Nihon Chūō* (Center of Japan) with the tip of his
bow. But it is said to have existed farther north, in Tsubo
Village, in today's Aomori Prefecture: hence the name
"Tsubo." It was this one to which Saigyō referred in a poem:

    Mutsunoku no oku yukashiku zo omohoyuru Tsubo no Ishibumi
    Soto no Hama kaze
    Deep in deep Mutsu I can't help thinking quietly: the
    Tsubo Stone Marker and the Outer Beach wind

This legend itself makes the existence of the marker suspect.
In the second place, the marker that is supposed to have
been dug out on the Taga Castle site and then was touted as
a great archeological find carries inscriptions that are doubt-
ed to have originated in the days of Taga Castle because of
their calligraphic style and their content. Thus, it is probable
that the marker in Sendai is a double hoax.

11   It seems that Bashō did compose a hokku in Matsushima,
for the following haibun has survived.

Matsushima is the best scenery in Japan, I'm told. People past and present, concentrating their poetic minds on these islands, have devised ways and employed art. The sea area is about three square *li*, where various islands of unusual shape look as if exquisitely chiseled by a heavenly artist. Each with pine trees flourishing on it, they are beautiful, splendid beyond description:

Shimajima ya chiji ni kudakete natsu no umi
Islands have shattered into a thousand pieces in the
    summer sea

Interestingly, Tohō is the one who preserved this.

12 With this as hokku, a thirty-six-link sequence was composed. The first six links of the sequence, which had five participants, is translated below. Fūryū is a pen name of Shibuya Jimbei (dates unknown). There is nothing known about Soei.

Suzushisa o waga yado ni shite nemaru kana   —BASHŌ
Making the coolness our home we lie about

tsune no kayari ni kusa no ha o taku   —SEIFŪ
to repel mosquitoes as always I burn grass

kanoko tatsu onoe no shimizu ta ni kakete   —SORA
the clear water from the fawn-hill led to the paddies

yūzuki marushi ninomaru no ato   —SOEI
evening moon is round above the second donjon site

nara momiji hitokage mienu shō o oto   —SEIFŪ
oak crimson: no one around but the sound of the *shō*

mozu no tsure kuru iroiro no tori   —FŪRYŪ
a shrike has brought various birds

After a typical salutatory exchange between guest of honor

and host, Sora turns the eye to a larger landscape outside. The fawn indicates summer. Soei then changes the season to autumn by mentioning the moon, which, normally, should be mentioned in the fifth link. The description of a ruined castle suggests something from the past, so Seifū brings in an ancient musical instrument, the *shō*. The mention of the *shō* suggests the sharp calls of a shrike. . . .

Bashō had another thirty-six-link session with Seifū, along with Soei and Sora.

13   With the initial version of this hokku, a thirty-six-link renga was composed in the house of Takano Ichi'ei, with two other participants: Sora and someone identified as Sensui.

> *Samidare o atsumete suzushi Mogami-gawa*   —BASHŌ
> Gathering May rains and cool, the Mogami River

> > *kishi ni hotaru o tsunagu funagui*   —ICHI'EI
> > on the bank, boat-poles moor fireflies

> *uri-batake izayou sora ni kage machite*   —SORA
> at the melon patch I wait for the sixteenth-day moon

> > *sato o mukai ni kuwa no hosomichi*   —SENSUI
> > a village beyond a narrow mulberry path

After another typical salutatory exchange—Bashō thanking the host for providing such a refreshing spectacle and Ichi'ei apologizing that the place he supervises is so godforsaken that the boat-poles, intended to moor boats, can only attract fireflies—Sora "brings up" the mention of the moon by two links to suggest something vaguely romantic. Then Sensui switches the viewpoint from something near ("the melon patch") to something far ("a village beyond"). In Sora's link, "the melon patch" indicates summer. In Sensui's, "mulberry" may appear to specify a season but it does not; this link belongs to the "miscellaneous" category.

14 With one of the two earlier versions, a thirty-six-link sequence was composed with a total of eight participants, including Egaku. The first three:

Arigata ya yuki o kaorasu kaze no oto ———BASHŌ
Admirable: the sound of wind making the snow fragrant

 sumu hodo hito no musubu natsukusa ———ROGAN
 summer grass made into a living space

 kawafune no tsuna ni hotaru o hikitatete ———SORA
 fireflies on the riverboat rope add to the scene

In this opening, Sora denies Rogan's self-deprecation by saying that the beauty of the abode they have been provided with is enhanced by fireflies. Sora switches the scene but also extends Bashō's compliments.

15 A thirty-six-link sequence that Bashō and Sora did with Shigeyuki and Rogan. The first four links:

Mezurashi ya yama o iDeha no hatsu nasubi ———BASHŌ
Surprise: coming out of the mountain and this first
 eggplant

 semi ni kuruma no oto souru ido ———SHIGEYUKI
 added to cicadas, the wheel's noise at the well

kinu-hata no kure isogashiu osa uchite ———SORA
the silk-loom busy at evening, the shuttle flying

 uru'u-yayoi mo sue no mikazuki ———ROGAN
 intercalary third month ends with a crescent moon

Bashō's hokku—which puns on Dewa, a place name that contains the element of the word *deru*, "to exit" (hence my peculiar transliteration)—compliments the host. He, along with Sora, has just come out of a religious training ground and, look, is at once offered the chance to savor the season's first eggplant! Shigeyuki, in a self-deprecatory gesture, says that his place is such an unrefined place that on top of the noisy cicadas there are the squeaks of the bucket wheel at the well. Sora expands Shigeyuki's description to include the noise of a shuttle. Rogan switches the viewpoint to describe the sky.

16 The thirty-six-link sequence with this as hokku was composed with three participants: Bashō, Fugyoku, and Sora.

Atsumi-yama ya Fuku-ura kakete yūsuzumi —BASHŌ
From Mount Atsumi away to Fuku Bay: evening cool

miru karu iso ni tatamu ho-mushiro —FUGYOKU
on the kelp-harvesting shore straw mat sails folded

tsuki ideba sekiya o karan sake motte —SORA
with moon rising, let's rent a barrier hut to have a drink

In response to Bashō's compliments, Fugyoku deprecates himself by noting a bleak scenery where washed-up kelp is harvested and fishermen are so poor that they can afford only straw mats in place of regular cloth sails. To counter the self-deprecation, Sora brings up the Taoist notion—while also bringing up the moon by two links—that to enjoy oneself in destitution is an elegant thing to do, for what is implied by *sekiya*—the residential quarters for barrier guards—is something less than sumptuous.

17 An incomplete sequence of seven links—with the wealthy merchant Terashima Hikosuke (dates unknown) and six other participants— begins with the earlier version of this hokku. Here are the first two links.

Suzushisa ya umi ni iretaru Mogami-gawa —BASHŌ
How cool: the Mogami River pours into the sea

tsuki o yurinasu nami no uki-miru   —HIKOSUKE
floating kelp makes the moon waver

Bashō's revision here is another example where the change makes the hokku far more effective as an independent poem.

18   An incomplete sequence of twenty links with this as hokku, with eight participants, remains.

Fumitsuki ya muika mo tsune no yo niwa nizu   —BASHŌ
Seventh month: even the sixth isn't like an ordinary night
tsuyu o nosetaru kiri no ichiyō

—Ishizuka Kiemon SAGURI
a single paulownia leaf with dew on it

This is an example where the hokku and waki do not contain elements of salutation between guest of honor and host.

19   Bashō apparently did not do a renga sequence with this celebrated hokku, but later wrote a haibun with the title, *Ode to the Galaxy:*

From the place called Izumozaki in the province of Echigo, Sado Island, it is said, is eighteen *li* away on the sea. With the cragginess of its valleys and peaks clearly visible, it lies on its side in the sea, thirty-odd *li* from east to west. Light mists of early fall not rising yet, and the waves not high, I feel as if I could touch it with my hands as I look at it. On the island great quantities of gold well up and in that regard it is a most auspicious island. But from past to present a place of exile for felons and traitors, it has become a distressing name. The thought terrifies me. As the evening moon sets, the surface of the sea becomes quite dark. The shapes of the mountains are still visible through the clouds, and the sound of waves is saddening as I listen.

Araumi ya Sado ni yokotau Amanogawa
Rough sea: lying toward Sado Island the River of Heaven

20 A combination of a poet and a prostitute recalls a witty exchange of tanka between Saigyō and a prostitute named Tae, which Saigyō noted took place in the seaport town of Eguchi:

> Once, when I paid my respects to Ten'nō Temple, it suddenly began to rain, so I tried to seek lodging in Eguchi but was refused, and I made this poem:

> *Yononaka o itou made koso katakarame kari no yado o mo*
> *oshimu kimi kana*   —SAIGYŌ
> To spurn this world may be difficult, I know, but you
> even refuse me temporary lodging

> In reply:

> *Yo o itou hito to shi kikeba kari no yado ni kokoro tomuna to*
> *omou bakari zo*   —PROSTITUTE TAE
> Having heard you've spurned this world I only hope
> you won't think of temporary lodging

Because of this enlightened response, the legend was born that Tae was in truth Fugen Bosatsu, the Bodhisattva of Universal Virtue. The nō play *Eguchi*, attributed to Kan'ami (1333–84), is based on this exchange and the legend born of it.

Aside from this literary allusion, the question arises what Bashō might have meant to suggest through the pairing of the bush clover and the moon. Did he mean to compare the prostitutes to the bush clover, himself to the moon? If he did, might that be condescending or didactic? Or did he mean to suggest haikai in the pairing itself, which was rare in court poetry and therefore was "humorous"?

21 The session was held at the house of the Shinto priest Fujimura Izu, whose haikai name was Kosen:

Shiorashiki na ya komatsu fuku hagi susuki —BASHŌ
Daintily-named Little Pine blowing bush clover,
pampas grass

tsuyu o mishirite kage utsusu tsuki —KOSEN
knowing the dew the moon casts its light

odori no oto sabishiki aki no kazu naran —HOKUSHI
the sound of a dance: aspect of lonesome fall

As guest of honor, Bashō compliments the elegance of
the place. Kosen, as host, compares Bashō to the moon. The
dance Hokushi refers to may be part of a harvest festival.

22 The sequence, with three participants, was probably com-
posed not on the twenty-seventh of the seventh month,
when Bashō visited Komatsu, but when he came back there
in the early part of the following month:

Ana muzan ya na kabuto no shita no kirigirisu —BASHŌ
Oh, how cruel: under the helmet a cricket

chikara mo kareshi tsuyu no akikusa —KYŌSHI
strength faded on the dewy autumn grass

watashimori tsuna yoru oka no tsukikage ni —KOSEN
a ferryman makes a rope in the hillside moonlight

Here the customary salutation is omitted.

23 Bashō has left a haibun, *Ode to the Hot Spring*. The hokku
used here is an earlier version:

After traveling along the beach of the Northern Sea, I
bathed in the hot spring of Yamanaka, in Kaga
Province. A villager said, "This is one of the three
greatest hot springs in Japan." Certainly, as I bathed
often, my skin and flesh were moisturized, muscles
and bones softened, heart and mind relaxed, and I

truly felt my complexion revived. I did not care whether the boat to the earthly paradise or the marker for Tz'u-t'ung's chrysanthemums was lost.

Yamanaka ya kiku wa taoraji yu no nioi
In Yamanaka I'd never break mums off in hot water's scent

24 At the beginning of the *Yūgao* (Moonflower) chapter are the following descriptions. Koremitsu is Daini's son:

While still making secret calls near Sixth Avenue, Genji said, "My wet nurse, Daini, has fallen gravely ill and become a nun. I must inquire after her," and went to visit her at her house, on Fifth Avenue, to rest on his way from the Palace.

Because the gate through which his carriage was to enter was locked, he had Koremitsu summoned and, while waiting, looked at the avenue, which was none too appealing. Next to Daini's house was a fence of cypress wood newly made, and above it were four or five shutters raised, with blinds that were very white and gave a cool appearance. Through them Genji could see a number of women with pretty foreheads looking out. They seemed to be standing about, and as he thought of the rest of their bodies, he had to decide they were unusually tall.

"What kind of people have gathered there?" he wondered, realizing how different their lives must be from his. He had brought an extremely plain carriage; he also had brought no runners.

"Who would know who I am?" he said to himself, relaxing somewhat and peering into the women's house. Its gate had something like a shutter pushed up, and it was a shabby house with barely yard space behind the gate. He was touched, but as he reflected, "Which place can I say?" it seemed no different from a jeweled palace.

On a fence-like thing crawled a very green vine contentedly and a single white flower had opened up as if smiling.

"To someone over there I say this," he said to himself. His attendant knelt down and said, "That white-blooming thing is called 'moonflower,' sir. The name of the flower suggests a woman, but it tends to bloom on miserable fences like this."

The attendant was right. All around this unappealing place where the houses tended to be small, each and every one of them weirdly leaning and dilapidated, all the eaves, which did not at all look solid, had moonflowers crawling over them.

"I pity their fate. Pick one for me," Genji said.

His attendant went inside the raised gate and picked the flower. Despite the appearance of the house, a pretty girl wearing a longish, yellow, unlined skirt made of silk came to the somewhat elegant sliding door and beckoned. Then she gave him a heavily incensed white fan, saying, "Why don't you put the flower on this and give it to the gentleman? The vine of the flower isn't that presentable, you know."

Genji later finds out that a poem addressed to him is written on the fan. His remark, "Which place can I say?" alludes to an anonymous tanka in *Kokin Shū* (no. 987):

Yononaka wa izure ka sashite waga naramu yuki tomaru o zo yado to sadamuru
In this world, which place can I say is mine? Wherever I end up I'll call it my inn

This poem is a meditation on the transience of life and says that there is no permanent abode for any human being. Recalling this poem, Genji decides that, be it a shabby house or a jeweled palace, it is all the same.

Another remark of his, "To someone over there I say

this," alludes to an anonymous 5–7–7, 5–7–7-syllable *sedōka* in *Kokin Shū* (no. 1007):

Uchiwatasu ochikatabito ni mono mōsu ware
sono soko ni shiroku sakeru wa nani no hana zo mo
To someone I see over there I say this:
"What kind of flower is it that blooms white there?"

25   The account reads:

It appears to have been Priest Saigyō who, enamored by the view of the sea at Kehi, moved to see the colors of Colored Beach and left for us a keepsake, a poem about small *masuho* shells. As a result, even the smallest patch of land around here keeps speaking his name, soothing the heart of anyone with a poetic turn of mind who wanders between the tides. Over the years I had thought of coming over here, but now Bashō Tōsei, of Edo, has come to this beach by way of touring a number of provinces. Invited on the same boat, I have picked small shells, wrapped them in my sleeves, and put them in a cup, so I might relive the days of that famed priest.

WRITTEN BY TŌSAI, OF FUKUI, ECHIZEN

Ko-hagi chire masuho no kogai ko-sakazuki   —TŌSEI
Small bush clover, fall: small *masuho* shells in a small cup

26   *Hamaguri no futami ni wakare yuku aki zo* is the most haikai of all the pieces included in *Oku no Hosomichi*.

Hamaguri, "clam," is mentioned first as a compliment because Ise is known for good clams. The word *futami* is a multiple pun meaning "lid and flesh," "two bodies," "to see the lid," and the place name Futami, a cove in Ise Bay famous for the "husband-and-wife" rocks and which, following the standard Chinese characters applied to it, itself means "two views." In court poetry, *Futami no Ura* (Futami

Cove) is often preceded by the epithet *tama-kushige*, "jeweled box," obviously because *futa* of Futami means "lid"; so, to present the inelegant clam as a pseudo-epithet was haikai. (The initial version, made on the ferry, had *futami e*, which, because *e* is a directional specifier, makes the reference to the cove stronger.)

If the meaning of "to see the lid" is stressed, the "lid" here may refer to the *gekū*, "the external shrine," at Ise. Unlike the *naikū*, "the internal shrine," which houses the Sun Goddess, the *gekū* houses Princess Toyuke, the goddess of food and industry. For some reason, Bashō skipped the ceremony for installing the new buildings at the *naikū*, which took place on the tenth of the ninth month, but attended the corresponding ceremony at the *gekū*, which took place on the thirteenth. Bashō made a hokku on that occasion as well:

Tōtosa ni mina oshiainu go-senkū
Awestruck: all jostling one another at the rebuilding

In grammatical construction, *hamaguri no* can be the modifier of Futami, as has been noted; in that case, the sentence subject, which is unstated, can be Bashō or he and his friends who are heading for Futami Cove to visit Ise Shrine. But *hamaguri no* can also serve as the sentence subject, as is clear from my translation.

Yuku, "go," has a double function: *wakare yuku*, "go separate ways," and *yuku aki*, "autumn that is going away." Bashō's reference to *yuku aki*, "departing autumn," brings us back to *yuku haru*, "departing spring," in the second hokku of this travel account.

Finally, Bashō probably remembered what Saigyō had written on Futami Cove:

> In Futami Cove, of Ise, I saw girls apparently from good families gathered, collecting clams in what appeared to be a voluntary fashion. I would have understood it if they were

miserable fishermen, so told them that it was beneath their state to do such a thing. They answered that they were collecting and selecting clams because someone in Kyoto asked for them for seashell-matches. So I made this poem:

Ima zo shiru Futami no Ura no hamaguri o kai-awase tote
ōunarikeri
Now I know: they cover the clams at Futami Cove,
saying it is for seashell-matches

Seashell-matches or *kai-awase* is a game in which 180 pairs of clam-shell halves are divided into groups and then matched. Initially they were plain; later, to make the matching easier, suitable pictures were painted on them or upper and lower hemstitches of tanka were written on them.

A Farewell
Gift to Sora

PREFATORY NOTE

WHEN SORA WAS PREPARING TO CUT HIS TRAVELS WITH Bashō short because of his stomach trouble, he, along with Bashō and Hokushi, whom the two travelers met in Kanaza-wa, did a haikai sequence, although evidently he had to leave mid-way through it. Hokushi published it two years later, in 1691, in *Udatsu Shū,* but in 1839, a version retaining some of the phrases before Bashō changed them, as well as Bashō's comments and some alternative links—apparently Hokushi had jotted them down—was brought to light in *Yamanaka Shū.* Since then the annotated version has been known as *Sora Sen: Okina Naoshi no Ikkan* (A Farewell Gift to Sora: A Scroll Corrected by Bashō). It is one of the few sequences illustrating the way Bashō worked as a haikai master. The sequence itself, without annotation, is also known as *Yamana-ka Sangin* (A Sequence by Three Poets in Yamanaka), *Tsubame Kasen* (Swallow Kasen), or, taking the first phrase of the hokku as is often done, *Uma Karite* (Renting a Horse).

Aside from the disjunctive narrative mode and the role of the hokku that I detailed in the Introduction, the following may be counted among the more important rules of the renga:

- All individual descriptions fall in one of the six thematic cat-egories: the four seasons, love, and miscellaneous—the last sometimes subdivided into "religion" and other themes.

- The 36-link sequence is divided into 6, 12, 12, and 6. The first half is called the *sho'ori,* "first fold," and the second the *nagori no ori,* "remaining fold." Each "fold" is then divided into an *omote,* "front," and a *ura,* "back." So, the first 6 links are called the *sho omote,* the 12 links that fol-low the *sho ura,* the next 12 the *nagori no omote,* and the last 6 the *nagori no ura*. These names derive from the way a sheet of paper is folded.

- Certain movements, such as *jo-ha-kyū* (introduction, development, finale), are assigned to the overall structure.

- Three links are set aside for the description of the moon, which represents autumn, the 5th, 14th, and 29th, with a fourth description optional; and 2 links for the "flower" (cherry blossoms), which represents spring, the 17th and the 35th. These positions may be changed, though the second mention of the flower tends to remain in the designated place. (Reference to a flowering plant other than the cherry, as happens in the second link in the sequence that follows, does not make the link a "flower" link.)

- A description of spring or autumn must last at least for 3 consecutive links but not more than 5, except at the very end of the sequence, where 2 links are acceptable.

- A description of summer or winter may not last for more than 3 consecutive links.

- Similar descriptions may not occur with 1 link in between.

- The final part, called the *ageku*, must be congratulatory.

In the translation that follows, lines taken to be remarks rather than descriptions are put in quotation marks. There seldom is a clear distinction, however, and the choice is mostly arbitrary.

A FAREWELL
GIFT TO SORA

SHO OMOTE (FIRST FRONT)

1   *Uma karite tsubame oiyuku wakare kana*   —HOKUSHI
Renting a horse you follow the swallows as we part

2   *hanano midaruru yama no magarime*   —SORA
a field of flowers disturbed where the mountain turns

3   *tsuki yoshi to sumō ni hakama fumi-nugite*   —BASHŌ
"The moon's good": they kick off their hakama for wrestling

4   *saya-bashirishi o yagate tomekeri*   —HOKUSHI
sword running out of its scabbard stopped in a flash

5   *aobuchi ni uso no tobikomu mizu no oto*   —SORA
into the blue depths an otter jumps the water sound

6   *shibakari kokasu mine no sasa-michi*   —BASHŌ
he fells brushwood along the hilltop's bamboo-grass path

7   *arare furu hidarino yama wa Suge no tera*   —HOKUSHI
"On that hail-falling mountain to the left is Sedge
Temple"

8   *yūjo shigo-nin inaka watarai*   —SORA
four or five prostitutes making the rounds of the
countryside

9   *rakugaki ni koishiki kimi ga na mo arite*   —BASHŌ
"Among these graffiti is the name of someone I love"

10   *kami wa soranedo uo kuwanunari*   —HOKUSHI
he hasn't shaven his head but doesn't eat fish

11   *hasu no ito torumo nakanaka tsumi fukashi*   —SORA
"Making thread from lotus is itself a sinful thing"

12   *senzo no hin o tsutaetaru mon*   —BASHŌ
ancestral poverty lives on in this house

13 *ariake no matsuri no kamiza katakunashi*   —HOKUSHI

under a daybreak moon the ceremony's top seat is
obstinate

14   *tsuyu mazu harau kari no yumi-take*   —SORA

dew first brushed aside for bamboo to make a
hunting bow

15 *akikaze wa mono iwanu ko mo namida nite*   —BASHŌ

in the autumn wind even the silent child is in tears

16   *shiroki tamoto no tsuzuku sōrei*   —HOKUSHI

white sleeves go on and on at the funeral rite

17 *hana no ka wa furuki miyako no machi zukuri*   —SORA

flower scent and town construction in the ancient City

18   *haru o nokoseru Genjō no hako*   —BASHŌ

spring lingers on Genjō's box

NAGORI NO OMOTE (REMAINING FRONT)

19 *nodokasa ya Shirara Naniwa no kai-zukushi* —HOKUSHI
serenity: seashell collections of Shirara, Naniwa

20 *gin no ko-nabe ni idasu seri-yaku* —SORA
in a small silver pot he serves broiled parsley

21 *temakura ni shitone no hokori uchi-harai* —BASHŌ
arm for a pillow he brushes dust off his princely bed

22 *utsukushikare to nozoku fukumen* —HOKUSHI
hoping for a beauty he peers into the mask

23 *tsugi-kosode takimono-uri no kofū nari* —BASHŌ
in a quilted kimono he's an incense vendor of the old
style

24 *hikuraudo naru hito no kikuhata* —BASHŌ
once a junior chamberlain, now in his chrysan-
themum patch

25 *shigi futatsu dai ni suete mo sabishisa yo* —HOKUSHI
even two snipes offered on a tray, wanting

26 *aware ni tsukuru mikagetsu no waki* —HOKUSHI
movingly he makes a waki on the crescent moon

27 *sho-hosshin kusa no makura ni shugyō shite* —BASHŌ
an acolyte sleeping on a grass-pillow for training

28 *Obata mo chikaku Ise no kamikaze* —BASHŌ
Obata is close by, and Ise's divine wind

29 *hōsō wa Kuwana Hinaga mo hayari sugi* —HOKUSHI
"The smallpox has already peaked in Kuwana, Hinaga"

30 *ame hare kumori biwa tsuwaru nari* —HOKUSHI
"Rain, sun, or cloud, the loquats ripen"

NAGORI NO URA (REMAINING BACK)

31 *hosonagaki sennyo no sugata taoyakani* —BASHŌ
the slender figure of a goddess full of grace

32 *akane o shiboru mizu no shiranami* —BASHŌ
wringing the madder in the water, waves white

33 *Nakatsuna ga Uji no ajiro to uchi-nagame* —HOKUSHI
Nakatsuna views it all as the weir of Uji

34 *tera ni tsukai o tateru kōjō* —HOKUSHI
message for which a courier's dispatched to a temple

35 *kane tsuite asoban hana no chirikakaru* —BASHŌ
I'll ring the bell for fun as flowers scatter on me

36 *sukyōnin to yayoi kureyuku* —BASHŌ
a zany and a March day in the growing dark

IN THE COMMENTS BELOW, FOR WHICH I AM GREATLY INDEBT-ed to Nose Tomoji and Shimasue Kiyoshi, the reasons given for the changes Bashō made are, of course, guesswork. With this understanding, locutions such as "probably" and "is thought to have meant" are omitted.

SHO OMOTE (FIRST FRONT)

1   *Uma karite tsubame oiyuku wakare kana*   —HOKUSHI
     Renting a horse you follow the swallows as we part

> Autumn. Kigo: swallows. The ailing Sora rented a horse and headed south, the direction to which swallows were now returning. Swallows, when described in a setting that suggests their "coming," are a kigo for spring, and so is their nest, whereas swallow chicks are a kigo for summer.
>
> This hokku is salutatory in expressing the sadness of parting in an open, natural way. There is no comment by Bashō.

2   *hanano midaruru yama no magarime*   —SORA
     a field of flowers disturbed where the mountain turns

> Autumn. Kigo: a field of flowers. Sora returns the salutation, suggesting that he will disappear from view where the road turns at the skirt of the mountain. His original version was *hanano ni takaki iwa no magarime*, "a field of flowers where a tall boulder turns." Bashō made the change because Sora's phrasing was some-

what flat in sentiment and attracted too much attention to "a tall boulder." "Disturbed" also refers to the departing person's state of mind.

3 *tsuki yoshi to sumō ni hakama fumi-nugite*   —BASHŌ
"The moon's good": they kick off their hakama for
wrestling

Autumn. Kigo: moon ("brought up" from the normal position by two links). Bashō originally had *tsuki haru-ru,* "with the moon clear," for the first five syllables. He made the change to accommodate the change in the waki: to avoid a similar phrasing (*midaruru* and *haruru*) and to make the focus of the action sharper. *Hakama* are formal pantslike garments worn by men and suggest young samurai. A switch is skillfully made from day to night and from people bidding farewell to people preparing to wrestle.

4   *saya-bashirishi o yagate tomekeri*   —HOKUSHI
         sword running out of its scabbard stopped in a flash

Miscellaneous. Hokushi originally wrote *tomo no,* "by a friend," instead of *yagate,* "in a moment." Bashō said the original phrase was "heavy." The introduction of a definite human figure either cluttered the overall image or made the action too explanatory. Several months later, in the fourth month of 1690, he wrote to Miyazaki Shikin (1673–1735) and his brother Sensen (d. 1706) and urged them to "try not to be heavy-handed and roundabout in haikai and hokku." His emphasis on *karumi,* "lightness," in his final years probably took shape during this period.

A sword, if tilted in the wrong way when not fastened with a ferrule, easily runs out of its scabbard and can be dangerous. A sword sliding out in that manner is a metaphor for an impetuous, impudent man.

This and the preceding links evoke the scene describing a round of sumo wrestling matches during a banquet following a hunt in *Soga Monogatari* (The Tale of the Soga Brothers), a story of a vendetta that took its present shape in the fourteenth century. The matches ended when one man "grabbed the sword his page was holding, slid it [out of the scabbard], and confronted" another.

5 *aobuchi ni uso no tobikomu mizu no oto* —SORA
 into the blue depths an otter jumps the water sound

Miscellaneous. Bashō mulled this over and suggested changing the first five syllables to read *nisan biki,* "two or three [otters]." But after a while he said, "'Into the blue depths' is just fine," and went back to Sora's original.

 If Sora and Bashō felt anything about this verse in relation to Bashō's famous hokku about a frog or frogs jumping into a pond, it is not known. On the other hand, *uso,* here given as "otter," also means "lie," as in "to tell a lie," so this line can be a parody.

6 *shibakari kokasu mine no sasa-michi* —BASHŌ
 he fells brushwood along the hilltop's bamboo-grass
 path

Miscellaneous. In working this out, Bashō thought of using *tadoru,* "to follow," or *kayou,* "to frequent," instead of *kokasu,* "to fell." With the former word, the meaning becomes "a brushwood gatherer follows the hilltop's bamboo-grass path," and with the latter, "brushwood gatherers frequent the hilltop's bamboo-grass path." He decided against either one, because neither has the immediacy of the original word that corresponds to the sound of an otter jumping into the water.

7   *arare furu hidarino yama wa Suge no tera*   —HOKUSHI
     "On that hail-falling mountain to the left is Sedge Temple"

Winter. Kigo: hail. Hokushi's initial version had *matsu fukaki*, "pine-deep," for the first five syllables. Bashō changed it to carry forward the sense of movement indicated by *kukusu*, "to fell."

Suge no tera, "Sedge Temple," is said to refer to Kanzan Temple, in Ōmi, which is closely associated with the Sugawara family, the most famous member of which is Michizane (845–903). *Suge*, *kan* (of Kanzan), and *suga* (of Sugawara) all use the same Chinese character meaning "sedge."

Placing *mine*, "hilltop, peak," in the preceding link and *yama*, "mountain," so close together may violate the rule that frowns on describing two similar things in proximity.

8   *yūjo shigo-nin inaka watarai*   —SORA
     four or five prostitutes making the rounds of the
     countryside

Miscellaneous. Sora had *yakusha*, "actors," instead of *yūjo*, "prostitutes." Both are traveling people making a wretched living, but prostitutes evoke more pity in the cold weather suggested by "hail-falling," as well as compassion associated with a temple. Prostitutes in earlier traditions had some entertainment skills, such as singing.

If Bashō associated Sedge Temple with the Sugawara family, this link may refer to the following scene in *Sarashina Nikki*, a diary by the Daughter of Sugawara Takasue (1008–60).

What is called Mount Ashigara was terrifyingly dark for four or five *li*. Even in the foothills we finally reached, we could hardly see the sky. The trees luxuriated in indescribable fashion and were truly terrifying. We lodged in the foothills; it was a moonless, dark night and you felt as if lost in the darkness. Still, three playgirls appeared out of nowhere. One of them was about fifty, another about twenty, and a third in her midteens. They spread a parasol and set it up in front of our hut. Our male servants lit torches to see them better. They said they were the grandchildren of someone who was once known as Kohata. Their hair was extremely long and covered their foreheads elegantly. White in complexion, they did not at all look grubby. People pitied them, saying they could easily be maids at an imperial house. As the women sang their admirable songs, their voices rose limpidly into the sky, incomparably.

Here the author is recalling the travels to Kyoto she made with her family when she was twelve years old.

This link prepares the way for a description of "love."

9   *rakugaki ni koishiki kimi ga na mo arite*   —BASHŌ
    "Among these graffiti is the name of someone I love"

Love. Bashō initially had *koshibari ni* for the first five syllables; *koshibari,* "hip-pasting," is the paper pasted on the lower part of a wall or a sliding door and suggests an inn where prostitutes are staying. Ihara Saikaku (1642–93), a prolific haikai and prose writer at whom Bashō looked askance, refers to just such an amorous graffito on a *koshibari* in Book II of *Kōshoku Ichidai Otoko* (The Life of an Amorous Man). Bashō changed it to make the effect less specific, less *busy.*

The link is translated as if it were a remark by one of

the prostitutes. The meaning of the link can be more general, "Among these graffiti are the names of loved ones."

10   *kami wa soranedo uo kuwanunari*   —HOKUSHI
         he hasn't shaven his head but doesn't eat fish

Miscellaneous (Buddhism). Bashō praised Hokushi for "grasping the heart" of the preceding link. Hokushi's description suggests someone who has decided to take Buddhist vows by becoming a vegetarian—Buddhism proscribes consumption of anything sentient—but whose resolve to enter priesthood is not firm enough to shave his head. This link's connection to the preceding one is that the person still has an attachment to love and other worldly matters. Also, linked to this, the preceding link suggests someone who discovered that he had unconsciously written the name of his lover while dawdling.

11   *hasu no ito torumo nakanaka tsumi fukashi*   —SORA
     "Making thread from lotus is itself a sinful thing"

Summer. Kigo: lotus. (If the Buddhist sentiment of this description is emphasized, this link can be in the "Miscellaneous" category.)

Bashō also praised Sora for this one. Making thread out of lotus pod fiber refers to the legend of Princess Chūjō, who is said to have woven a mandala out of such thread. Sora's link says that making thread out of the lotus, a plant sacred for Buddhists, is a pious act, but that when viewed from the absolutist Buddhist dogma it too is a sinful thing.

Together with the preceding link, this can be part of a monologue: "I haven't tonsured myself but don't eat fish. Still, I can't brag about it. When you think of it, even making thread out of the lotus to make a mandala, as Princess Chūjō is said to have done, is extremely sinful."

12   *senzo no hin o tsutaetaru mon*   —BASHŌ
      ancestral poverty lives on in this house

Miscellaneous. Bashō first had *shigo-dai*, "four or five generations," instead of *senzo no*, "ancestral." One reason for the change is obvious: the phrase, "four or five," is used in the eighth link. Another reason is that "ancestral" is larger in concept, strengthening the irony of the observation. The relation of this link to the preceding one is that someone who regards as sinful the pious act of making thread out of lotus pods is likely to be at best an eccentric who, probably because of his considerable pedigree, flaunts the family tradition of destitution.

13   *ariake no matsuri no kamiza katakunashi*   —HOKUSHI
      under a daybreak moon the ceremony's top seat is obstinate

Autumn. Kigo: daybreak moon—("brought up" by one link). Hokushi's initial version read: *yoizuki ni matsuri no jōdai katakunani*, "under the evening moon the ceremony adheres to the old ways." In the revised version, the general meaning is retained, with *kamiza*, "top seat, the seat of honor," denoting the person sitting there.
    Bashō made the change from "evening moon" to "daybreak moon" because the daybreak, suggesting a prolonged all-night ceremony, is more appropriate for such a person and occasion.

14   *tsuyu mazu harau kari no yumi-take*   —SORA
      dew first brushed aside for bamboo to make a hunting
      bow

Autumn. Kigo: dew. Linked to the thirteenth link, this suggests someone who, early in the morning, is looking for fine bamboo with which to make a ceremonial hunting bow. But the linking factor is tenuous, with only the similar atmospheres created to make the connection possible. Tenuousness in linking was not discouraged; some renga masters argued such linking would be far superior.

15 *akikaze wa mono iwanu ko mo namida nite* —BASHŌ
in the autumn wind even the silent child is in tears

Autumn. Kigo: autumn wind. With the introduction of a child who doesn't say anything, the preceding link is made to suggest a poor hunter or a masterless samurai.

Hokushi reports that when he told Bashō this link was excellent, Bashō returned the compliment, saying both Hokushi and Sora had written links equally good.

16   *shiroki tamoto no tsuzuku sōrei* —HOKUSHI
white sleeves go on and on at the funeral rite

Miscellaneous. A different reason is given for the child's tears. In those days white was the color for funerals. It was also the metaphoric color for autumn. (See note 299.)

17 *hana no ka wa furuki miyako no machi zukuri* —SORA
flower scent and town construction in the ancient City

Spring. Kigo: flowers—a mention of cherry flowers is required here. Sora originally had *hana no ka ni Nara no miyako no machi zukuri,* "amid the scent of flowers town construction in the City of Nara." Bashō's revision makes the description less specific and more suggestive. With or without Bashō's revision,

Sora, with a reference to cherry flowers, succeeds in switching the subject from something funereal to something flowery.

18   *haru o nokoseru Genjō no hako*   —BASHŌ
        spring lingers on Genjō's box

Spring. Kigo: spring. Genjō, the first son of Satomura Jōha (1524–1602), wrote orthodox renga, rather than haikai no renga. Genjō himself died young, in 1607, but in 1617 the Satomura family was officially employed by the Tokugawa government for renga instruction, and in 1628 was put in charge of the annual renga session with the shogun participating. Held on the twentieth of the first month, it was a perfunctory, ceremonial affair with the hokku and the third link prepared beforehand by two representatives of the family. These sessions, along with the renga composed for them, were symbolic of the stultification of orthodox renga.

The Satomura family, in any case, was originally from Nara. "Genjō's box" suggests the meticulously crafted, lacquered kind in which things like "secret transmissions" were kept. What is intended here is an atmosphere of traditional elegance.

NAGORI NO OMOTE (REMAINING FRONT)

19   *nodokasa ya Shirara Naniwa no kai-zukushi*   —HOKUSHI
        serenity: seashell collections of Shirara, Naniwa

Spring. Kigo: serenity—*nodokasa* suggesting the balmy, languid atmosphere of a typical spring day.

Hokushi initially had *kai ōshi,* "many seashells," for the last five syllables. Bashō's change is subtle but vital, for if you say "many shells," the link becomes a description of beaches—which both Shirara and Naniwa are—

whereas if you say *zukushi,* "showing all the varieties in one category," the focus shifts to the box. *Zukushi* was common in books, illustrations, and paintings, and, here, it could allude to the design on Genjō's box, even the seashells inlaid on it.

20   *gin no ko-nabe ni idasu seri-yaku*   —SORA
        in a small silver pot he serves broiled parsley

Spring or winter. Kigo: broiled parsley. In response to the preceding link that suggests an old-fashioned elegance, Sora introduces a "small silver pot," hinting at a person of refined taste with a certain eccentricity. He then fulfills the expectation by mentioning "broiled parsley," a recipe thought to be especially *sabi*—the quality of being elegant in deprivation. Parsley was actually cooked in a pot, but this recipe dictated that the vegetable be described as "broiled," giving it a sophisticated touch.

Sora apparently left soon after writing this link, for this is the last time he appears in the sequence. Bashō, enchanted by this description, thought up two possible links and, deciding that the beginning phrase of both, *temakura ni,* "arm for a pillow," would be a good connecting image, urged Hokushi to try to work out his own links. By Bashō:

temakura ni omou koto naki mi narikeri
arm for a pillow, he's someone with nothing to
    worry about

temakura ni noki no tama-mizu nagame wabi
arm for a pillow, watching beads of water from the
    eaves, alone

Hokushi came up with two:

temakura no yodare tsutōte mezamekeru
arm for a pillow, drool dribbling, waking

temakura ni take fuki wataru yūmagure
arm for a pillow: a wind blows through bamboo at
dusk

Finally, Bashō decided to use the following, another of
his own:

21   *temakura ni shitone no hokori uchi-harai*   —BASHŌ
arm for a pillow he brushes dust off his princely bed

Miscellaneous. Bashō rejected the four possibilities
because they all had some problems. His first is too
abstract. His second suggests a court lady watching the
melting snow drip from the eaves and is appropriately
elegant. But it can cause some technical problems. If
"broiled parsley" is taken to represent the category of
spring, this link would continue the same season for
five consecutive links or the maximum allowed. If, on
the other hand, "broiled parsley" is taken to belong to
the category of winter, that would mean dropping the
season of spring and returning to it only after one link
on a different season, a practice not allowed. Hokushi's
first possibility suggests a low-class servant, making its
connection to the preceding link difficult; and his sec-
ond, though not bad, is not elegant enough.

The version Bashō decided to use, in contrast, sug-
gests a man of Proustian languor, thereby putting the
man of the preceding link in sharper focus. (For a
poem combining "pillow" and "dust," see the section
quoted from *Izayoi Nikki* in the Introduction, p. 32.)
Also, Episode 140 of *Yamato Monogatari* (Tales of
Yamato), a tenth-century compilation of poetic tales,
reads in its entirety:

> While the late Prince, the Minister of Military
> Affairs, lived with Major Councilor Noboru's
> daughter, he used to lay his bed not in the usual
> bedroom but on the verandah. After he left the

place, he did not come back for a long time.
Then he sent her an inquiry, "Is the bed I laid in
the verandah left as it was? Or did you remove
it?" In reply, she said:

*Shikikaezu arishi nagara ni kusa-makura chiri nomi zo
iru harau hito nami*
I haven't changed it, have left it as it was, only dust
on your grass-pillow with no one to brush it off

In reply, the prince said:

*Kusa-makura chiri harai niwa karagoromo tamoto yuta-
ka ni tatsu o matekashi*
Wait to brush the dust off my grass-pillow until
I make ample Chinese-robe sleeves

Again, in reply:

*Karagoromo tatsu o matsu ma no hodo koso wa waga
shikitae no chiri mo tsumorame*
While I wait for you to make a Chinese robe,
dust will go on piling up on my bedroom
sheet

So the prince came to visit her, but then went
off, saying, "I'm going hunting in Uji." In
response, the woman said:

*Mihari suru Kurikoma-yama no shika yori mo hitori
nuru mi zo wabishikarikeru*
More than the deer you hunt on Mount Kuri-
koma, I, sleeping alone, feel the pain

The "late Prince" is Motoyoshi (890–943) and the
major councilor, Minamoto no Tōru (848–918). The
"grass-pillow" is a metaphor for traveling, so the refer-
ence to it by Yuzuru's daughter is a complaint that
Motoyoshi did not regard his affair with her as more
than temporary. Motoyoshi's poem refers to the cus-
tom of spreading on the floor the sleeves of each

other's clothes for sleeping together. *Karagoromo,* "Chinese robe," is a *makura-kotoba,* an epithet that modifies words related to clothing such as *tatsu,* "to make," *kiru,* "to wear," and *tamoto,* "sleeve."

22   *utsukushikare to nozoku fukumen*   —HOKUSHI
        hoping for a beauty he peers into the mask

Love. Prompted by the reference to a bed, Hokushi suggests a prostitute summoned by the languid man of the preceding link. In the old days women often wore masking hoods when they went out. Ryūtei Tanehiko, a pen name of the samurai Minamoto no Tomohisa (1783–1842), is known to have written a tract illustrating all such masks for women popular at the time.

23   *tsugi-kosode takimono-uri no kofū nari*   —BASHŌ
      in a quilted kimono he's an incense vendor of the old style

Love. *Tsugi-kosode,* here translated "quilted kimono," are comparable to quilts; they started out as utilitarian objects, but went on to become fashionable items. By Bashō's time they had become something that reminded one of the good old days. The "incense vendor" here is a male prostitute. In Book II of *Kōshoku Ichidai Otoko* (see link 9), Saikaku describes such prostitutes; Yonosuke the amorous man associates with three men of the same sexual preference "day and night" and goes bankrupt. In light of this, the person whose face was peered into in the preceding link becomes a pretty boy disguised as a woman.

After several more links were written, Bashō came back to this link, and said that *kosode* here and *shitone* in the twenty-first link suggested things too similar to each other, but that he couldn't come up with any alternative.

24   *hikuraudo naru hito no kiku-hata*   —BASHŌ
once a junior chamberlain, now in his chrysanthemum
  patch

Autumn. Kigo: chrysanthemum. As sometimes hap-
pens when only two persons write a sequence, Bashō
writes two consecutive links from now on to avoid
monotony. For the same purpose, one of the two par-
ticipants may alternate two links and one.

A *hikuraudo*, "junior chamberlain," worked at the
court as an apprentice to a chamberlain. Usually from
a good family, he was allowed the privilege of en-
tering the court's inner quarters, but his low rank
was fixed; someone given this title sometimes per-
formed female servants' work. Bashō's description
suggests such a junior chamberlain now retired and
cultivating chrysanthemums for pleasure. With this,
the "incense vendor" in the preceding link becomes a
true incense vendor trying to sell his wares to a man
of leisure.

Hokushi noted a technical question he confirmed
with Bashō in relation to this link. It had to do with
the rule that when three consecutive links describe
people (rather than, say, landscapes), the atmosphere of
the third link must be very different from that of the
first, and the person described in the third link must
sharply contrast with that of the second.

25 *shigi futatsu dai ni suete mo sabishisa yo*   —HOKUSHI
even two snipes offered on a tray, wanting

Autumn. Kigo: snipes. The offering can be either to
the retired junior chamberlain or from him. Either
way, the suggestion is that a normally respectable gift
looks shabby in the presence of someone with an aris-
tocratic air. Bashō praised Hokushi for this transition.

26   *aware ni tsukuru mikagetsu no waki*   —HOKUSHI
   movingly he makes a waki on the crescent moon

Autumn. Kigo: crescent moon ("brought up" by three
links). Hokushi was reminded by the preceding link of a
renga session, which usually had dining as part of its
proceedings. (One notice for haikai sessions that Bashō
is said to have had pasted on his wall said, among other
things, "Be content with whatever cheap food and
cheap tea you may have" and "Don't get drunk and
rowdy.") Hokushi notes that Bashō said, "There could
also be a link like this," but what that comment meant is
not clear.

27 *sho-hosshin kusa no makura ni shugyō shite*   —BASHŌ
   an acolyte sleeping on a grass-pillow for training

Miscellaneous (Buddhism). Bashō initially had *tabine
shite*, "sleeping while traveling," for the last five sylla-
bles. He changed it because it is redundant to combine
kusa no makura, "grass pillow," a standard metaphor for
going to sleep while traveling, and *tabine*, which says
exactly what the metaphor means. Even after the revi-
sion, he said with a laugh, "This sort of link may be
found in any sequence." He thought it was a *yariku*, an
easy or quick link chiefly meant to keep it going.

When connected to the preceding link, at any rate,
this link suggests a man new to religious ways who has
put up at an inn and joined a renga session.

28   *Obata mo chikaku Ise no kamikaze*   —BASHŌ
    Obata is close by, and Ise's divine wind

Miscellaneous (Shintoism). Obata is an area just across
a river from the Grand Shrine of Ise. Coupled with the
preceding link, this one suggests a man who has trav-
eled to pay homage to the shrine and, now finding

himself close to it, is touched by a waft of wind from that direction. The "divine wind" refers to the special wind from the Grand Shrine, told of in the *Kojiki* and *Man'yō Shū*, which is supposed to help those on the side of justice.

29 *hōsō wa Kuwana Hinaga mo hayari sugi* —HOKUSHI
"The smallpox has already peaked in Kuwana, Hinaga"

Miscellaneous. Both Kuwana and Hinaga are place names in Ise. The suggestion is that the raging smallpox couldn't come too close to the Grand Shrine. Bashō praised Hokushi for his adroitness in employing the *yotsude* ("four hands") technique that describes two items in response to two items in the preceding link— here, two place names set against two place names.

30 *ame hare kumori biwa tsuwaru nari* —HOKUSHI
"Rain, sun, or cloud, the loquats ripen"

Summer. Kigo: loquats. Hokushi originally had *hito ame goto ni*, "with each rainfall," for the first seven syllables. The connection of this link to the preceding one is the changeable weather when smallpox tended to occur.

NAGORI NO URA (REMAINING BACK)

31 *hosonagaki sennyo no sugata taoyakani* —BASHŌ
the slender figure of a goddess full of grace

Miscellaneous. A *sennyo*, a woman who has acquired magical powers, suggests the legendary world of China, recalling, in relation to the preceding link, the story about a woman who, after spending a night with a king and bidding farewell, said she would henceforth appear over the nearby hill "as a cloud in the morning and as a rain in the evening." Another explication refers to the ancient Chinese use of loquat leaves as divine medicine.

Hokushi says Bashō smiled contentedly when praised for the excellence of this link. Nevertheless, the annotator Nose says the linking of this description to the preceding one is not clear to him.

32   *akane o shiboru mizu no shiranami*   —BASHŌ
      wringing the madder in the water, waves white

Miscellaneous. Standing alone, this suggests a woman washing red madder-dyed cloths in a river, in some areas a common sight in those days. But when coupled with the preceding link, it turns the immortal goddess in the preceding link into a mortal female. Bashō painted with words a picture of a Chinese goddess that Kitagawa Utamaro (1753–1806) might have drawn with a brush. The transition from the thirty-first link to the thirty-second, along with the humor generated, is considered excellent.

33 *Nakatsuna ga Uji no ajiro to uchi-nagame*   —HOKUSHI
    Nakatsuna views it all as the weir of Uji

Winter. Kigo: weir. Minamoto no Nakatsuna (1126–80) was one of the generals who participated in the battle at the Uji River, in 1180, the first important confrontation between the rebelling Minamoto clan and the ruling Taira clan. According to *The Tale of the Heike,* to take the offensive the Taira commander Tomonori (1152–85) plunged all of his twenty-eight thousand warriors—a slight poetic exaggeration here— into the river famed for its rapid currents, causing havoc. Among the many warriors pushed downstream, three in bright red armor got caught in the fishing weir. Mindful that the fishing weirs of the Uji River were a favorite topic of court poets, Nakatsuna, when he saw the men, composed an impromptu tanka:

Ise musha wa mina hiodoshi no yoroi kite Uji no ajiro ni kakarinuru kana
Ise warriors, all clad in fire-frightening armor,
　have been caught up in the weirs of Uji!

Hokushi, in alluding to this episode in his link, gave a slight twist, lumping the warriors with the fishing gear. Bashō said, "This is another decoration in the sequence." He meant that the link was attractive, even though he no longer looked favorably on this type of obvious, fancy turn.

34　　　*tera ni tsukai o tateru kōjō*　　　　　—HOKUSHII
　　　message for which a courier's dispatched to a temple

Miscellaneous. Hokushi, following his own description, came up with an easy response. In the aforementioned battle, Mii Temple was an important backer of the Minamoto cause, and its leaders, warrior monks, and parishioners took part in the fighting. Indeed, following the Minamoto defeat, the temple, as well as the parishioners' houses, was set on fire by the Taira forces.

35　*kane tsuite asoban hana no chirikakaru*　　　　—BASHŌ
　I'll ring the bell for fun as flowers scatter on me

Spring. Kigo: flowers. When he came up with this link—the penultimate position that requires a mention of cherry flowers—Bashō said he also thought of saying *chiraba chire* for the last five syllables, which would have made the line mean, "I'll ring the bell for fun; flowers, scatter, if scatter you must!" He decided against it, he said, because it wasn't poetic enough *(fūryū nashi)*. It would also have followed the *Heike* story too closely—for three consecutive links.

Either way, the link recalls a famous tanka on spring by Priest Nōin in *Shin-Kokin Shū* (no. 116):

Yamazato no haru no yūgure kite mireba iriai no kane ni hana zo chirikeru

Coming to a mountain village in the spring
    evening, at the vesper bell, flowers scatter

The connection of the revised link to the preceding one is rather tenuous, except for the association of a temple with a bell. One possibility is that the mock-serious tone of the thirty-fourth link prompted Bashō to think of an eccentric.

36   *sukyōnin to yayoi kureyuku*   —BASHŌ
        a zany and a March day in the growing dark

Spring. Kigo: third month—here given as "March"—the last month of spring by the lunar calendar. A translation more faithful to the syntax would be: "while people keep calling me a zany, the third month comes to a close." The phrase *kureyuku* means at once "to grow dark" and "to come to an end."

As he wrote this, the *ageku*, Bashō said to Hokushi that he simply described the person in the preceding link. Such a zany or an eccentric is, as we have seen, a favorite topic of haikai poetry. He added, "But be careful with an *ageku*." He meant that despite the tone in which he ended this sequence, one shouldn't often be as lighthearted at the ending where a more formal congratulatory tone is the norm.

INDEX OF POETS

THIS INDEX PROVIDES REFERENCES TO POETS WHERE POEMS
are cited. Parenthesized numbers refer to notes, bracketed numbers to misattributions.

Abutsu, 31–32

Bashō. *See* Matsuo Bashō
Butchō, 55

Chōtarō,135

Fugyoku, 147
Fujiwara no Michimasa, 82
    (166)
Fujiwara no Sanekata, 137
Fūryū, 144

Gyōson, 100 (233)

Hikosuke, 148
Hokushi. *See* Tachibana
    Hokushi

Ichi'ei. *See* Takano Ichi'ei
Izumi Shikibu, 86 (181)

Kajiwara Kagesue, 20
Kakobata Toyoaki, 52 (45)
Kasa no Iratsume, 84 (172)

Kasho, 112 (276)
Kawai Sora, 49, 51, 52 (45),
    59, 81, 87, 92 (202), 93,
    102 (236), 103, 107, 121,
    141, 144, 145, 146, 147,
    160–63, 166, 168–69,
    171–73, 175
Ki no Tsurayuki, 31
Kiyohara no Motosuke, 74
    (128)
Kobayashi Issa, 102 (242)
Kosen, 149
Kume no Asomi Hirotsuna,
    112 (272)
Kusakabe Kyohaku, 71
Kyōshi, 150

Li Ling, 120 (308)
Li Po, 80 (146)

Matsuo Bashō, 27–28, 40 (3),
    41, 43, 46 (31), 47, 51, 52
    (45), 53, 57, 59, 61, 62
    (76), 63, 65, 67, 69, 71, 73,
    87, 89, 91, 93, 94 (204),

95, 96 (218), 97, 101, 103,
107, 109, 113, 114 (283),
115, 117, 119, 121, 123,
124 (314), 125, 129, 131,
133, 134, 135, 140, 141,
142, 144, 145, 146, 147,
148, 149, 150, 151, 153,
154, 160–65, 167–68, 170,
172–74, 176–84
Minamoto no Sanetomo, 76
(131)
Minamoto no Shigeyuki, 80
(150), 94 (211), 126 (321)
Minamoto no Tōru, 142–43
Minamoto no Tōru's Daughter, 175
Minamoto no Toshiyori, 44
(23), 70 (102), 86 (183)
Minamoto no Yorimasa, 48
(32), 58 (67)
Motoyoshi, 175
Murasaki Shikibu, 72 (109)

Nijōin Sanuki, 74 (127)
Nintoku, 84 (169)
Nōin, 19, 58 (66), 68 (95),
104 (246)

Ōtomo no Yakamochi, 84
(168), 112 (271)

Po Chü-i, 76 (130)

Ren'nyo, 122 (310)
Rissai. See Yanai Yasaburō

Rogan, 146
Rosen, 136, 144

Sagami, 84 (170)
Sagara Izaemon, 62 (76), 141
Saguri, 148
Saigyō, 42 (11), 56 (62), 60
(74), 68 (93), 82 (156),
[123], 130 (332), 143, 149,
154–55
Seifū, 144
Sensui, 145
Shigeyuki, 146
Sōchō, 24
Soei, 144
Sōgi, 25
Sora. See Kawai Sora
Su Tung-p'o, 80 (147)
Su Wu, 120 (306)

Tachibana Hokushi, 124
(314), 150, 160–67, 169,
171–75, 178–83
Tachibana no Suemichi, 70
(98)
Tae (Prostitute), 149
Taira no Kanemori, 58 (64)
Takano Ichi'ei, 28, 145
Teiji, 107
Tōkyū. See Sagara Izaemon
Tu Fu, 42 (13), 78 (145), 91

Yamaguchi Sodō, 82 (156)
Yanai Yasaburō, 62 (76)
Yūsei, 80 (153)

Other Titles from Stone Bridge Press
in the Rock Spring Collection of Japanese Literature

Death March on Mount Hakkoda by Jirō Nitta

Wind and Stone by Masaaki Tachihara

Still Life and Other Stories by Junzō Shōno

Right under the big sky, I don't wear a hat by Hōsai Ozaki

The Name of the Flower by Kuniko Mukoda

CONTEMPORARY JAPANESE WOMEN'S POETRY
A Long Rainy Season: Haiku and Tanka
Other Side River: Free Verse

Hōjōki: Visions of a Torn World by Kamo-no-Chōmei

Naked: Poems by Shuntarō Tanikawa

Milky Way Railroad by Kenji Miyazawa